No10 Downing Street

The Story of a House

N^o^10 Downing Street

The Story of a House

Christopher Jones

BRITISH BROADCASTING CORPORATION

Published by the British Broadcasting Corporation
35 Marylebone High Street, London W1M 4AA

ISBN 0 563 20441 9

First published 1985

Book design: Douglas Whitworth

Printed in Great Britain by Butler & Tanner, Frome
Colour printed by Chorley & Pickersgill, Leeds

CONTENTS

10 DOWNING STREET

THE PRIME MINISTER

All Prime Ministers are intensely aware that, as tenants and stewards of No 10 Downing Street, they have in their charge one of the most precious jewels in the nation's heritage. It is a heritage which every Prime Minister guards with care and affection. Each has tried to improve the old and charming house to suit the day's needs, while preserving, above all, its sense of history - and its sense, too, of being a private house where they and their families can lead their own lives, even among the intense and demanding activity of national and international politics.

How much I wish that the public - the people, after all, on whose behalf No 10 exists - could see beyond that famous front door, could share with me the great enjoyment that I am now privileged to derive from the elegant rooms of the house. How much I wish, too, that they could share with me the feeling of Britain's historic greatness which pervades every nook and cranny of this complicated and meandering old building. Alas, that cannot be, but I am delighted that, through the medium of this book, with its many photographs and pictures of the house both past and present, they will at least be able to see the delightful interior which lies behind that modest facade, and they will be able to capture the sense of continuity and dignified authority that gives No 10 its very special place in our national life.

<u>JULY 1985</u>

S. Jemes Parke
Charingcrosse
The Courte gate
The Courte
Preuy bridge
Kinges streate
A
Westmynster hall
Starre Chamber
The Queenes bridge

CHAPTER ONE
Before Mr Chicken

The last mere mortal to live at No. 10 Downing Street was Mr Chicken. On 22 September 1735 the demi-gods and goddesses of British politics moved in. They have been living there, on and off, ever since.

Mr Chicken is notable only for his odd name, and his total obscurity. He was, presumably, a tradesman or craftsman in a fairly prosperous way of business since he lived in a house – or at least in part of it – that was large and expensive. For nearly a thousand years people had lived and worked in the area, selling their skills and their wares to the Royal court that sprawled over Westminster and Whitehall. After he moved out, No. 10 was repaired and improved, and was then offered as a gift by George II to his principal minister, Sir Robert Walpole. Sir Robert, however, would accept it only as the official residence of the First Lord of the Treasury, and to this day it is occupied by the Prime Minister only in his or her capacity as the First Lord.

That area at Westminster has always been at the centre of the nation's life. Around the narrow lane that was eventually to become Downing Street the King's court grew, and even before then ordinary people made their lives there, and believed they saw wonders and mysterious things.

Downing Street is on the edge of what was once called Thorney Island – simply, the Island of Thorns – a thirty-acre site that was formed between two branches of the river Tyburn, which flows down from the Hampstead Hills to the Thames at Westminster. The Thames river was wider then and sluggish, and at about the point where Westminster Bridge now stands there was a ford, which met the Roman road that came up through Kent from the Channel ports. On the stony and marshy ground of Thorney Island the Romans established some sort of settlement, and there they built a temple to Diana. Round about the temple, small homesteads grew up on the desolate ground. When work was being done on extensive rebuilding at Downing Street in the 1960s, broken pieces of Roman Samian pottery, from the second century AD, were found in a rubbish pit beneath the courtyard of No. 10.

According to legend, it was to the misty and mysterious Thorney Island that St Peter came on one stormy night to found the church

Whitehall and Westminster, *c.* 1560. Downing Street was to be built to the left of the gate at the top of Kinges streate

that was eventually to become the Abbey Church of St Peter. Above the noise of the storm the Thames ferryman at that spot, Edricus, heard a traveller calling him from the far shore of the river. Edricus reluctantly made the double journey over the swollen river to bring the heavily-cowled figure across to Thorney Island. There the stranger went into the small wooden chapel that some early Christians had already built in that place, and as he entered, all the candles in the place sprang into flame, and choirs of angels sang. The stranger then revealed himself, to an awe-struck Edricus, as the great Apostle Peter himself, and on that spot the Abbey was eventually to rise. That, at least, was the story that the monks at the Abbey were later to tell the credulous pilgrims since a suitable miracle was enough to draw the faithful – and their money – away from the rival St Paul's, just down the river.

Here too, at Westminster, on Thorney Island, the wise Danish King Canute built his royal palace, and here – or so one version of the legend says – he commanded the waves of tidal Thames to obey him. But 'the Thamas, unacquainted with this new god, held on its course, flowing as of custome it used to do and refrained not to assayle him neere to the knees'. The point being – and a point still to ponder among the mighty in Downing Street so near to the place in which this story happened – not that the King thought he was powerful enough to hold back the tide, but that his flattering courtiers were made to look the fawning fools that they were.

Whitehall Palace, mid-16th century. Sketch by Anthony van den Wyngaerde. The Cockpit is in the middle at the back

Edward the Confessor had his great palace here at Westminster, too, and William the Conqueror and his son built there massively, laying the true foundations for Westminster to become the seat of government. *Domesday Book* in 1086 describes Westminster as a 'manor within the hundred of Ossulston in Middlesex, belonging to the Church of St Peter'. The estate had only twenty-five houses, and the fence which surrounded most of it had a gate where Downing Street now joins Whitehall. The abbot

of the same place holds thirteen hides and a half. There is land to eleven ploughs . . . The villanes have six ploughs, and one plough more may be made . . . Pasture for the cattle of the village. Pennage for one hundred hogs. And twenty-five houses of the knights of the Abbott and of their vassals, to pay eight shillings a year. Its whole value is Ten Pounds; the same when received; in King Edward's time Twelve Pounds. This manor was and is in the demesne of the church of St Peter of Westminster.

So the area round Downing Street was a completely rural scene, with grazing cattle and rooting pigs scattered among the peasants' hovels. The palace, of course, just beyond the walls surrounding the fields, grew in increasing splendour, and the local people prospered with it. By the middle of the twelfth century there were admiring records of the citizens' gardens, 'spacious and splendid, set about with trees'. As for the people who owned the gardens, they were 'everywhere known for their civil demeanour, their goodly apparel, their table and their discourse'.

The church of St Margaret grew up beside the Abbey to serve the needs of the local people. The Abbey was for the monks of the monastery and for the great royal occasions. St Margaret's was – and still is – the parish church for the people who live around Whitehall and in Downing Street, and it was dedicated to St Margaret of Antioch, who was swallowed by a dragon (or the Devil) which promptly disgorged her because the cross she carried irritated the creature's stomach! Behind the church and the Abbey, William Caxton set up his printing press in 1476, and there he produced the first printed document in England: an indulgence granted by the Abbot of Abingdon to a man and his wife who had contributed to the maintenance of the Christian fleet against the Turks. The ground on which Downing Street was to be built belonged to the same Abbey of Abingdon, and it was from its monks that the Crown obtained the site.

Some fifty years later, Henry VIII moved out of his great palace at Westminster, and in 1529 confiscated nearby York House from the disgraced Cardinal Wolsey. York House now became Whitehall, and around it Henry built the pleasure grounds that were essential to his lusty and energetic life. Four tennis courts were laid out – both covered and open – as well as a bowling green, a Cockpit (which was later to play a vital part in the development of Downing Street) and a Tiltyard, which was used for bear-baiting. Along the east side of Whitehall, beside the river, there was a large Privy Garden, complete with a central sundial, which extended right down to Palace Yard and Westminster Hall. Inns, shops and houses were knocked down to make way for the King's new buildings, but the Axe Brewery, on which No. 10 would eventually be partly built, remained to supply the Royal table with the necessary beer. Beside the Tiltyard – roughly on the site of the present-day Horse Guards – an elaborate gallery was built for the Princes 'with their nobility . . . to stand or to sit, and at Windowes to behold all the triumphant Iustings, and other military exercise'.

Two massive gates were built at the north and south ends of Whitehall Palace: the Holbein Gate at the north end; the New Gate, or King's Street Gate, at the south end, at the spot where Downing Street now runs into Whitehall. Beyond that, King Street – very roughly, the present Parliament Street – connected the Royal palace to Parliament at Westminster, although it was a mean and muddy thoroughfare, hardly fit for a royal procession, and the citizens of Westminster had to fill up the ruts with faggots before the king went, in state, to open Parliament. An Act of 1532 describes King Street as 'very foul and full of pits and sloughs, very perilous and noyous as well for all the King's subjects'.

Henry, for all his brutality, could be extremely delicate in his likes and dislikes. He was, for instance, offended by the sight of funeral processions going past his Palace to St Margaret's, so he had a new burial ground opened at St Martin-in-the-Fields. He also had the Leper Hospital, which had stood for three centuries on the edge of St James's Fields, surrounded with a brick wall – although he presumably did not object to the jollifications at the five-day Fair held each July to raise money for the lepers.

Queen Elizabeth I used the gallery that her father had built alongside the Tiltyard to watch the events that happened there – much as people in Downing Street today watch the Trooping of the Colour from their windows overlooking the same parade ground. But Elizabeth, uncharacteristically, was on one occasion caught off-guard while she watched the military exercises. Gilbert Talbot to the Earl of Shrewsbury, 3 May 1578:

> In the morning, about eight o'clock, I happened to walk in the Tiltyard, under the gallery where Her Majesty useth to stand to see the running at tilt; where by chance she was, and, looking out of the window, my eye was full towards her; she shewed to be greatly ashamed thereof, for that she was unready, and in her nightstuff; so when she saw me at dinner, as she went to walk, she gave me a great filip on the forehead, and told My Lord Chamberlain, who was next to her, how I had seen her that morning, and how much ashamed she was.

When the Queen rode in tremendous state, smothered in jewels, through the New Gate to open Parliament, the jewels had perhaps been made by Everard Everard, 'Goldsmythe et Jueler', who was one of the tenants of the Axe Brewery building which spread from the present-day Whitehall along the whole length of modern Downing Street to St James's Park. Both the New Gate and Holbein Gate, which connected the Tiltyard with the rest of the massive Palace, formed part of the great warren of rooms and apartments in which the courtiers lived. The Holbein Gate was much the more elaborate of the

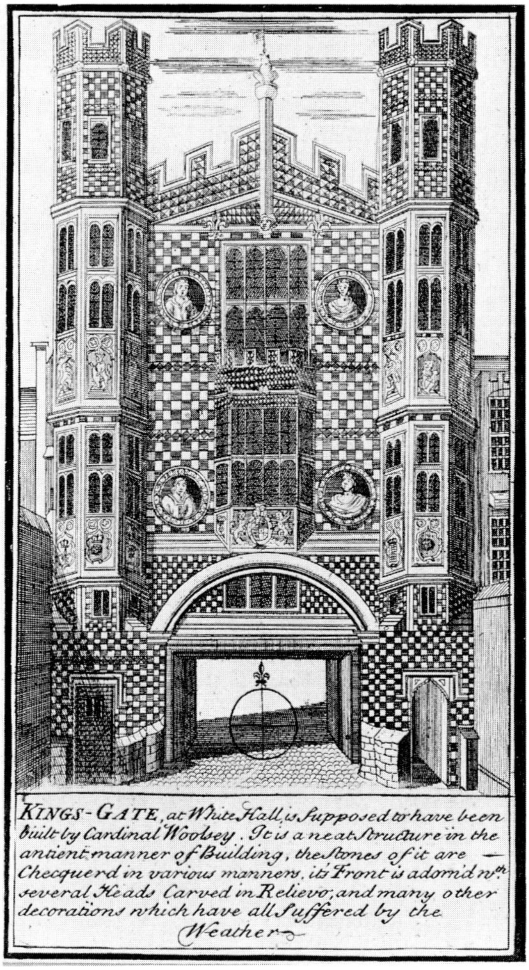

KINGS-GATE, at White Hall, is Supposed to have been
built by Cardinal Woolsey. It is a neat Structure in the
antient manner of Building, the Stones of it are —
Chequerd in various manners, its Front is adorn'd wth.
several Heads Carved in Relievo; and many other
decorations which have all Suffered by the
Weather

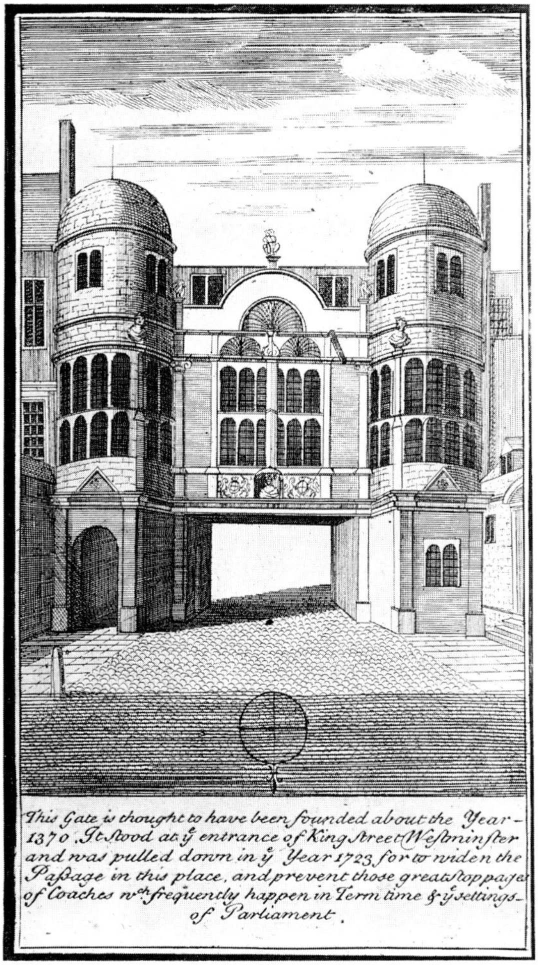

This Gate is thought to have been founded about the Year -
1370. It stood at ye entrance of King Street Westminster
and was pulled down in ye Year 1723, for to widen the
Passage in this place, and prevent those great Stoppages
of Coaches wch. frequently happen in Term time & ye settings -
of Parliament.

The so-called Holbein Gate (*above*) may have been called the King's Gate earlier. The King's Street Gate (*right*) stood roughly on the spot where Downing Street now joins Whitehall

two, with a complex chequered pattern set into its stonework, and plaques of classical heads decorating its towers. In later years it became more and more of an obstruction to the increasing traffic around Whitehall, and plans were made to pull it down. The great architect Vanbrugh was furious:

> I find many people surpris'd there should be no other expedient found to make way for coaches, &c., than destroying one of the greatest curiositys there is in London as that gate has ever been esteem'd, and cost a great sum of money the building; and so well perform'd that altho' now over 200 yrs old [*sic*], is as entire as the first day.

But progress had its way, and in 1759 the Holbein Gate was pulled down.

The King's Street Gate had already been demolished, perhaps because it made getting from Whitehall to the glossy new houses in Downing Street – or Downing Square, as it was sometimes called – difficult. It had had a colourful history. The Countess of Buckingham, mother of Charles I's favourite, lived there; 'twoe newe roomes' and much painting 'outsyde with redd oker twice over' were among the changes made for her, and she even entertained Jesuit priests there. 'The Countess of B's lodge, called the Porche, at the end of the King's garden, lodgeth three continually, to wit, Fisher, Walpole, and Floyd, besides two others that daily dine there, but lodge in the White Lion in King Streete, as I thinke, or els the Red.' Those five Jesuits would have dearly liked to make use of the Preaching Place in the royal Privy Garden nearby; although it would have been more than their lives were worth if they had tried. The Preaching Place was a wooden pulpit in the garden, where Archbishop Cranmer had harangued the young Edward VI, and which had turned that part of the garden into Sermon Court.

Other courtly grandees lived in the Gate after the Countess moved out, but by 1723 King's Street Gate had to go, and the entrance to Downing Street could be opened up. The Surveyor-General was directed to take custody of the 'keys of the Houses . . . on both sides of the Old Gateway in King Street', and 'immediately to proceed in pulling down the said Gateway entirely'. The materials were not to be 'taken as Fees, carryed away, or Purloyned', but sold for the King's profit.

In the constant building and rebuilding that went on in and around the Royal palace, another landmark which was to play an important part in the development of Downing Street had already disappeared. This was the Cockpit, which was demolished in 1675, and was part of the site on which the treacherous and wretched George Downing was able to run up his badly built row of houses. Over the years the original Cockpit had grown considerably, and had become a conglomeration of lodgings and offices. Cockfighting certainly took place there during James I's reign – the Treasury accounts had to meet the cost of 'Matt upon the cockpitt being broken and torne withe Cockes fighting there' – but later it became a playhouse and a hall for musical concerts.

James I was among the audience that watched the Children of Blackfriars perform a play there, and the whole place was elaborately decorated: 'Hatching and Guilding . . . with fine gold, and cullouring the great Braunches in front of the stage, and Hatching and Guilding all the parties to the seene forwards.' And even Oliver Cromwell unbent sufficiently to listen to a little music there. After a banquet in Whitehall for members of the House of Commons, 'His Highness withdrew to the Cockpit; and there entertained them with rare music, both voices and instruments, till the evening.'

Charles II, of course, made great use of the Cockpit for his court extravaganzas, and the first performance there after the Restoration of 1660 was of Ben Jonson's *Epicoene, or the Silent Woman*. 'Yesterday the King, Queen, Princesses, &c., supped at the Duke d'Albermarle's, where they had the Silent Woman acted in the Cockpit, where on Sunday he had a sermon.' It was on the Duke of Albemarle's lodgings in the Cockpit that the largest part of No. 10 Downing Street was eventually to be built.

The theatricals went on in the part of the Cockpit used as a playhouse. The dressing-rooms were hung with green cloth and there was 'one Looking Glasse of twenty seven Inches for the Women Comedians dressing themselves'. This mirror was necessary because 'the women have great difficulty in their dressing and such a glass too big to bee brought every night from their howse'. But the King's taste for elaborate spectacle meant the plays moved away from the Cockpit to the Banqueting Hall, and gradually the place became dilapidated. It became more and more unsafe, and in 1675 the playhouse was pulled down before it could collapse.

CHAPTER TWO

The House at the Front and the House at the Back

4 November 1605. The hands of the ancient clock in the tower in New Palace Yard were nearing midnight. A group of men hurried from the north door of Westminster Hall, crossed the Yard, and bustled along King's Street towards the King's Palace at Whitehall. They stumbled in the ruts and holes of the filthy road, as they made their urgent way through the pitch darkness – the lamps that citizens of Westminster had to hang outside their houses had been doused three hours before.

Guy Fawkes is seized by Sir Thomas Knyvet and others

As the men approached the gate that led from King's Street to Whitehall, they turned sharply left, hurried past the Cat and Bells tavern on the corner, and stopped in front of a stout oak door set in the middle of an imposing timbered house. They pounded on the door, and when it was eventually opened they demanded to see Sir Thomas Knyvet, the magistrate. As they waited for him to appear, the Clock in New Palace Yard struck midnight. 5 November 1605.

The men who had come to the magistrate's fine house were Lord Salisbury and Lord Monteagle; they had wind, they said, of a plot to blow up the King and his Parliament that very day. The three men, and their servants, hurried back to the Houses of Parliament, and there, in a room beneath the House of Lords, they found the wretched Guy Fawkes and his barrels of gunpowder all ready, as Fawkes was later defiantly to tell James I, to 'blow Scotsmen back to Scotland'.

Later that day, the Clerk of the House of Commons was to scribble, as an afterthought in the margin of the Commons Journal, the only Parliamentary record of the Gunpowder Plot:

> This last night, the upper house of Parlyam[en]t was searched by S[i]r Th. Knevett, and one Johnston serv[an]t to Mr Thomas Percye was there apprehended who had placed 36 barrelles of gunpowder in the Vawt under the house w[i]th a purpose to blowe K [the King] and the whole company, when they should be assembled. Afterwards div[er]se other gen[tlemen] were disciv[er]ed to be of the plott.

Sir Thomas Knyvet, the man who arrested Guy Fawkes, owned and lived in a house on the precise site of what is now No. 10 Downing Street.

Sir Thomas was a favourite of Queen Elizabeth I and had risen high among her court officials. He was a Gentleman of the Privy Chamber,

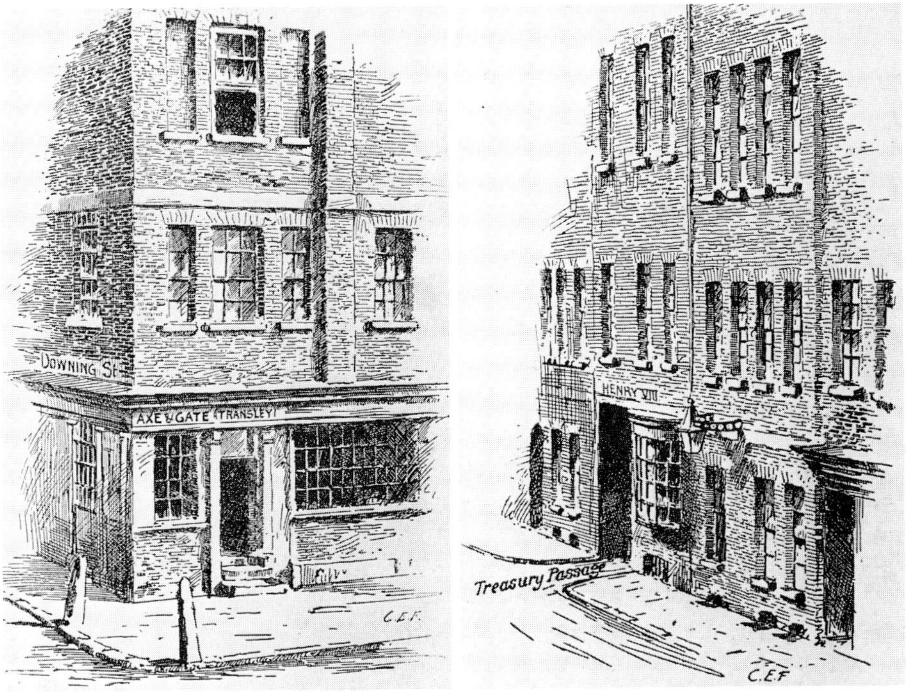

The Axe and Gate and (*right*) King Henry's Head taverns, Downing Street

and in 1581 had become the Queen's Keeper of the Palace; he was also to become the Member of Parliament for Thetford and a Justice of the Peace for Westminster. James I continued the royal patronage, and Knyvet was knighted at the Tower on 14 March 1604.

In the year that he became Keeper of the Palace, Elizabeth granted Knyvet the premises in what was to become Downing Street which had, for centuries, been used as a brewery. The Axe Brewery, which had belonged to the Abbey of Abingdon, was now in royal hands. Knyvet was given the property for life, rent free, and in May 1604 James I renewed and extended the arrangement so that Sir Thomas's heirs would keep the property for sixty years after his death. Again Sir Thomas had his fine house rent free, although he had already spent a considerable amount keeping it in good repair – the first, and most certainly not the last, of its tenants to find Downing Street a drain on his resources.

The house – called Knyvet House after its owner, in the manner of the day – was large and impressive. On the south side – the side, that is, nearest Westminster Abbey – the property was bounded by an inn listed as 'le Pecocke' and by the common sewer; on the north by 'le Newegate' leading to 'Kingesstreete' and passages leading to 'le Phesaunte le Courte' and to the great garden (the modern St James's Park); on the east by 'Kingesstreete'; and on the west by the wall to St James's Park.

In their leisure moments Sir Thomas and his wife would stroll out into the fields about their fine home, and watch the fireworks over the

Royal palace of Whitehall, or throw scraps to the animals kept in the Royal Zoo just behind the spot on which Downing Street now stands. There James I kept a leopard that the King of Savoy had presented to him; there were hawks and ermine from the Tsar of Muscovy, and antelopes from the Great Mogul. The King of Spain had sent camels and an elephant, and a couple of crocodiles kept the local urchins from risking a swim in St James's pond.

A pleasant life for the Knyvets, made still more amiable by the King's friendship. Lady Knyvet took especial care of the King's third daughter, Princess Mary, and on 4 July 1607 Knyvet was created Baron Escrik. By now an old man, he lived on another fifteen years, dying on 27 July 1622. He left most of his considerable property to his wife; his will is a touching tribute to her:

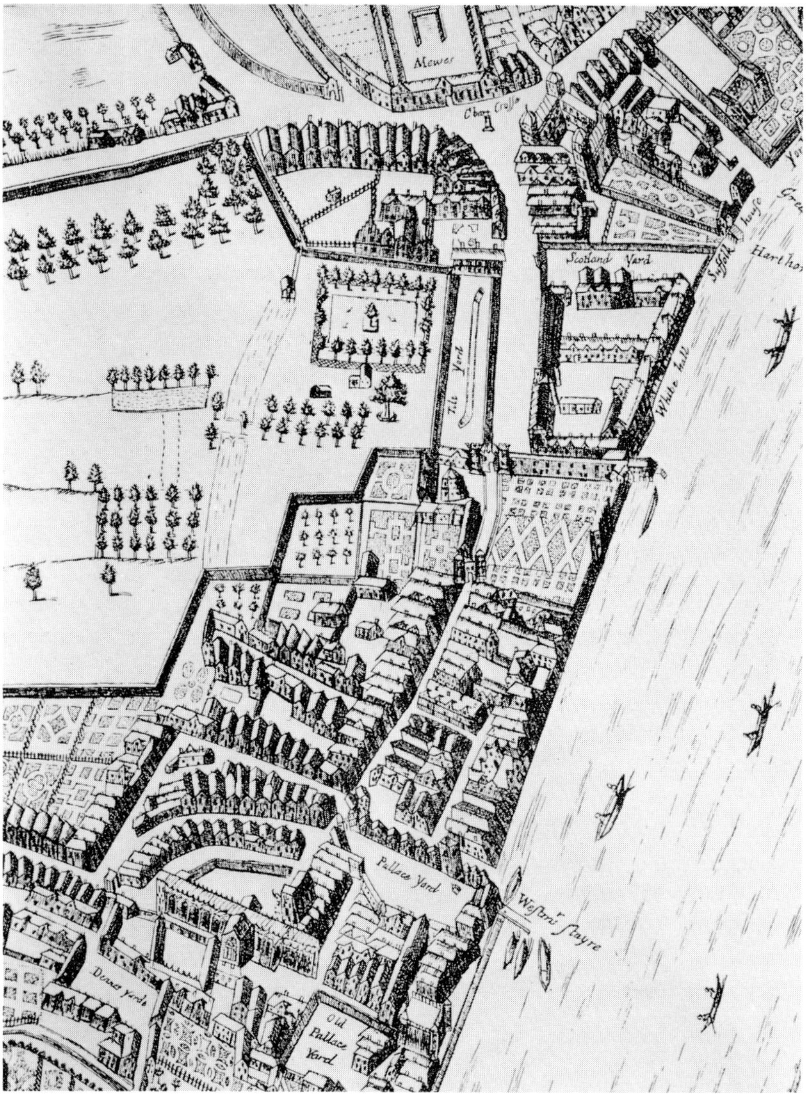

Westminster in 1658, by William Faithorne

Consideringe with my selfe that I was borne to nothing but a vaine title of blood and name of eminent freindes, and that the little fortune of my presente estat hath wholie risen by godes providence frm my deceased mother and my livinge and lovinge wife, by whose estat (though much wasted by me) I have been maynteyned, I hold myself bounde in civill honestie to . . . requitt her exceedinge true love . . . as much as shall lye in my power to doe yt.

But Knyvet's 'best deservinge and most dearly beloved wife' survived her husband only a few weeks. She died on 4 September 1622, within hours of making her own will in which she left the 'Downing St' property to her 'welbeloved Neece, Elizabeth Hampden, Widdowe'. Lady Knyvet added: 'And like as my late Lord and husband trusted me, Even soe doe I put my confidence in my said Neece.'

The trust was well placed, and Mrs Hampden was able to enjoy the property – it now became Hampden House – for forty years and to fend off the importunings of the wretched George Downing when he tried to get his hands on it. She was a formidable woman, a member of a tough political family. Her son was John Hampden, who fearlessly opposed Charles I over the imposition of Ship Money taxes, and who was one of the five Members of Parliament the King tried so disastrously and unsuccessfully to arrest in the House of Commons in 1642. Her nephew was Oliver Cromwell, the Lord Protector, who later had rooms in the Cockpit Chambers. After the Restoration in 1660, Mrs Hampden would have had to avert her eyes if she had gone to her parish church at St Margaret's, for on the roof of Westminster Hall, at the east end of the church, the Royalists had stuck her nephew's disinterred skull on a spike. But she stayed on in her fine house.

Mrs Hampden's property was substantial. In 1650 the Parliamentary Commissioners, who had taken over the Crown lands, described it as:

All that Messuage or Tenemt scittuate in King streete . . . built part wth Bricke and part wth Tymber and Flemish qalle and covered with Tyle, consistinge of a Large and spacious hall, Wainscoted round, well Lighted, and Paved wth brick Pavements, two parlrs whereof one is Wainscoted round from the seelinge to ye floore, one Buttery, one seller, one Large Kitchen well paved wth stone and well fitted and Joynted and well fitted wth dresser boords; Alsoe one Large Pastery Roome paved and ioynted as aforesaid. And above stayres in the first story one large and spacious dyneinge Roome, Wainscoted round from the Seelinge to the floore, well flored, Lighted and seeled, and fitted wth a faire Chimney wth a foote pace of Paynted Tyle in the same. Also 6 more Roomes and 3 Closetts in the same flore all well Lighted and seeled. And in the second story 4 garretts. And in annother Rainge of buildings called the old buildings Two Chambers and one Closett and a stoole house there, amd one Rainge of old buildinges standinge on the left hand comeinge in at ye gate, consisting of 9 roomes belowe stayres and above stayres. And on the Right hand of ye gate at the comeinge in to the said house one other buildinge standinge next to the streets, consisting of one Hall, one Kitchen, and a Closett, wherof one is parte wianscoted, and other parte fitted for hangings. Also one Court and two Large entryes or passages, & one large garden contayninge 252 feete of assize in length and 100 feete in breadth, the sd Large garden beinge fitted wth variety of Walle fruite & divers fruite Trees, Plants, Rootes and flowers, very pleasant to the Eye amd profitable for use. Alsoe severall handsom delightfull Gravelly Walkes, seats & arbors. the ground whereon th'aforesaid houses stand, together wth the Courts and garden, cont' by estimacon 397 feete of assize in Length, and ye garden 109 feete in breadth, & ye house 49 feete in breadth, abutting on Kinges Streete on the East, and St. James Parke walle on ye west, and adioyninge north of the New gate house leadinge into King streete, and south on a house or Inn heretofore called the Peacocke. now in ye occ. of Mrs Hampden, and is worth per annum £90.

This was the property that George Downing was determined to get hold of. In 1654 he eventually acquired what, before the Commonwealth was established, had been the Crown's interest in the property, but he could not actually get his hands on it since James I had given a lease to Knyvet which was to run for sixty years after his death – that is, until 1682. After the Restoration Downing successfully petitioned the King to be allowed to keep his interest in the property so he could rebuild there. 'His Maty, being graciously Pleased to gratify the Petnr in this his humble request,' directed the Lord Treasurer to arrange for a grant, with sufficient provision for 'the handsome and graceful building of the said house . . . the same standing so neere this Rll Pallace'.

Some of the Hampden property was, by then, in considerable disrepair – 'the houseing . . . are in great decay and will hardly continue to be habitable to the end', but Downing had to wait for nearly another twenty years before he could start rebuilding. His lease of 1663, however, allowed him eventually to build provided he did not go beyond the west part of the King's house at the Cockpit, but before he finally began to build, he persuaded the King to relax those restrictions. In 1681 Downing was granted permission to build new and more houses further towards St James's Park, provided they did not come nearer than fourteen feet to the park wall, and he had to cope the wall with free stone and 'set flowerpots and statues thereon'. Once the Knyvet lease ended in 1682 (Mrs Hampden had died in 1664 and left her interest in the property to her four grandchildren), Downing could finally go ahead.

The part of 10 Downing Street that was built on Downing's property forms the front, and most famous, section of the present-day house. The back – and by far the largest and grandest part – had nothing to do with that repellent man. The house-at-the-back was built on and around the old Cockpit lodgings, where the young Charles II had spent some of his childhood, and where Cromwell had lived for four years until his growing fondness for the trappings of Kingship – so enthusiastically encouraged by Downing – persuaded him to move into Whitehall Palace. The buildings that went up on the Cockpit site were to become a type of annexe to the Palace, and to be lived in by Royalty and their senior advisers before becoming the home of Prime Ministers.

The first of these grandees was George Villiers, the second Duke of Buckingham and a close friend of Charles II. He had been brought up with the Royal children, had fought in the Civil War, and at the Restoration became one of the most influential men at court. Eventually, with increasing alarm in the Commons at his influence, he fell from favour, leaving behind him at Westminster not only the ruins of a career but, apparently, the ruins of a house.

Buckingham had taken over his apartments at the Cockpit on the death of the Duke of Albemarle. Alterations were started in 1670. 'Charges in pulling downe & Altering severall Roomes at ye Cockepitt for his Grace the Duke of Buckingham' were listed, and in the autumn of 1671 there was 'covering wth lead ye Cantalaver Eaves and all ye hipps of ye roofe of ye new building'; and there was work, too, on '21 squares and 56 foote of Roofeing . . . 167 foote of lintelling . . . 10 oken Mantletrees and tassells . . . 74 window lights . . . 8 lucerne windowes . . .' The work went on until April 1673.

A splendid house indeed – but a decidedly rickety one. So rickety, in fact, that four years after it was built it had virtually fallen down: by May 1677 large-scale building was in hand on the same site. Perhaps it was destroyed by fire – although there are no records of this. Perhaps it suffered from the same problem that has bedevilled buildings at Westminster for centuries – the unstable ground of Thorney Island. Perhaps Downing's shoddy principles of jerry building had already spread to infect the Royal craftsmen.

Buckingham was by now 'living in retirement away from the Court', and his fallen-down house was rebuilt as a suitable residence for the King's daughter by the Duchess of Cleveland, Charlotte Fitzroy, and her new husband, the Earl of Lichfield. It is that house, into which the newly-married couple moved, that now forms the back part of No. 10.

Lady Lichfield was 'celebrated for her "blameless" beauty and her numerous issue', as well she might have been since she had eighteen children. She was married when she was twelve years old and her husband twenty. They settled down in what now became known as Lichfield House, and began producing their family. As the years went by, Mr Downing's speculative building on the edge of their property began to intrude on their privacy. Charlotte complained about it to her father, and on 3 April 1684 the King replied:

> I think it a very reasonable thing that other houses should not look into your house without your permission, and this note will be sufficient for Mr Surveyor to build up your wall as high as you please, the only caution I give you is not to prejudice the corner house which you know your sister Sussex is to have, and the building up the wall there will signify nothing to you, only inconvenience her.

That 'corner house' was roughly where No. 12 Downing Street, the Government Whips' office, now stands. The wall that Lady Lichfield got was, no doubt, very grand indeed, for 'Mr Surveyor' who was to be told to organise it was Christopher Wren.

But a wall by so great an architect was not cheap. Six months later Charles was writing to his daughter that 'I will give orders for the two hundred pounds for your building, and the reason that you have not had it sooner is the change I have made in my Treasury, which, now, in a little time, will be settled again, and so, my dear Charlotte, be assured that I am your kind father, C.R.'

Life continued amiably for the Lichfields in their fine house overlooking Horse Guards, but even such a great family had its small domestic dramas; from the *London Gazette*, 4–7 May 1685: 'Lost or

Plan of the house-at-the-back in 1677, showing the layout of the ground floor. 'Hambden Garden' is on the site of the present Downing Street; the garden surrounding the house still exists

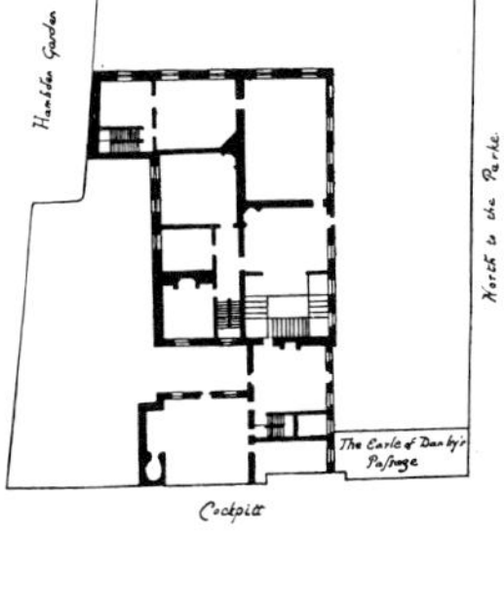

Left: The Earl of Lichfield, by Godfrey Kneller
Above: The Countess of Lichfield, mezzotint after Kneller

Stolen from the Earl of Litchfields House in St James's Park, upon 25th April last past, a little black and white Spaniel Bitch, having had one of her fore Leggs formerly broken which is now crooked.'

The Lichfields lived in the house until 1690, when Lord Overkirk moved in. He had started life as Henry Nassau, Count and Lord of Auverquerque, and had come to England with William III, when he assumed English nationality and an English spelling of his name. He was Master of the Horse to William and died in 1708, in his house listed as '*Overkirk* (the Lord) his House is situate in *Downing Str. Westminster*'.

The next tenant was another foreign nobleman. He made no attempt to become British but meddled a good deal in the country's affairs. Johann Caspar von Bothmar, Count Bothmar, came to England from Germany in 1710 as the envoy of the Elector of Hanover, the heir-presumptive to the English Throne who eventually became George I. Bothmar wielded very considerable influence over Queen Anne during the final years of her reign and became the 'virtual ruler' of her kingdom; and when George, who could not speak English, succeeded her, his influence remained as one of the 'Hanoverian Junta' which surrounded the King.

Such a grand and influential personage had, of course, to have a suitably grand house to live in. After Lady Overkirk died in 1720,

Count Bothmar, the Hanoverian envoy

Overkirk House became Bothmar House, and the builders were once again busy. They were working on 'finishing the Buildings, alteracions and repairs in the house in St James's park appointed for Count Bothmar'; and, among much else, their work included:

> The Back passage into Downing street to be repaired and a new Doore; a New Necessary House to be made; To take down the Useless passage formerly made for the Maids of Honour to goe into Downing Street, when the Queen lived at the Cockpitt; To New Cast a great Lead Cisturne & pipes and to lay the Water into the house & a new frame for ye Cisturne.

There, in his fine mansion, with its Necessary House and piped water, Count Bothmar lived until his death in 1732. Meanwhile the houses that Downing had developed on the site of Hampden House were now some fifty years old. They ran back-to-back with Bothmar House. Downing himself was long since dead, and had left instructions about his property in his will, mentioning particularly: 'My house in or neare King Street . . . lately called Hampden House, which I hold by a long Lease from the Crowne – and Peacock Court very neare adjoyning which I hold by lease from the Collegiate Church of St Peter, Westminster, all of which are now demolished and rebuilt or rebuilding and called Downing Street.' He listed, too, 'all those foure greate houses, being parcell of the premises held of the Crowne, fronting Saint James Parke West and North' – roughly the extent of today's Downing Street.

Downing left his very considerable estates to his sons, and they then passed to a grandson who was worthy of his thoroughly unprepossessing grandfather. The third baronet, also Sir George, 'never cohabited with his wife; & for the latter Part of his Life led a most miserable covetous & sordid Life'. He had one illegitimate daughter but most of his enormous wealth went, after a half-century of litigation, to the founding of Downing College, Cambridge. So, out of the last generation of the Downings there finally came some good; some reparation was badly needed, for the founder of their line had been one of the most contemptible figures in British history.

CHAPTER THREE
The Man Who Built Downing Street

The man who gave his name to Britain's most famous, most respectable, most desirable address was an infamous, treacherous turncoat. Pepys called him a 'perfidious rogue'; Andrew Marvell called him 'Judas'; and even the sedate *Dictionary of National Biography* says his reputation was stained by servility, treachery and avarice. He may not have been British; he was certainly educated in America – and then blamed America for his treachery. George Downing was Cromwell's spy-master and Charles II's fawning creature.

It is not known precisely when, or where, Downing was born. Perhaps it was in 1623 or 1625 in London, or perhaps it was at Mont Wealy, near Dublin, in 1624. It is, however, certain that his family came originally from East Anglia. His father was Emanuel Downing; his mother Lucy Winthrop, whose brother John was to become the first governor of Massachusetts. Both his father and his uncle were barristers at the Inner Temple, and both families were staunchly puritan. Not surprisingly, they found the political and religious atmosphere in England more and more unacceptable to them, and in 1630, ten years after the *Mayflower* sailed, John Winthrop set out on the ten-week journey to the New World.

Young George's father was keen to follow, but his mother was not. Mrs Downing obviously doted on her son – and her devotion was repaid, in later years, by his refusal to give her enough of his great wealth to allow her to live in comfort in her old age. She was, above all, worried about his education – he was, at one time, in school 'in Maydstone in Kent' – and she was sure that he could not get a proper training for the world if they, too, went to the wilds of unsettled America. Governor Winthrop urged his relatives to join him, but on 4 March 1637 Mrs Downing wrote to her brother putting off a decision. 'Poor boy, I fear the journey would not be so prosperous for him as I could wish, in respect you have yet noe sosieties nor means of that kinde for the education of youths in learninge: and I bless God for it he is yet reasonably hopeful in that waye.'

John Winthrop, Downing's uncle, the first governor of Massachusetts

In fact, plans were already going ahead in New England for the founding of a great university there. The 'gentle and Godly' John

Harvard, a Puritan minister and graduate of Emmanuel College, Cambridge, had left half his fortune and three hundred books for just such a purpose, and now the settlers decided to build their own college in their own new town of Cambridge. It was enough to persuade the Downings that New England was good enough for George, and they arrived there in October 1638. George pursued his studies with the Rev. John Fiske, and enjoyed himself in and around the town of Salem, shooting in the woods, bringing down the wild duck on Humphries' Pond, and fishing. And then, when he was possibly not quite sixteen, George Downing became the second graduate of the new Harvard University. Not long afterwards he was given a job at £4 a year at the college 'to read to ye Junior pupills as ye President shall see fit'.

But poor Mrs Downing's worries about her son continued. She had to sell off part of her property in England to pay for George's education, and complained to Governor Winthrop about her son's determination to leave her and travel. 'I perceive he is strongly inclined to travill. Eng. is I fear unpeaceable, and other countries perilous in poynt of religion and manners. Besides wee have not whearwith to acommodate him for such an occasion: and to go a servant I think not might be very fit for him neither in divers respects. . . . The good Lord direct him to His own glory.'

In spite of his mother's worries, George did in fact 'travill'. He had already studied divinity, and so in 1645, at the age of about twenty, he 'went in a ship to the West Indies to instruct the seamen'. His journey as ship's chaplain round the Caribbean was pleasant enough, and he so impressed the people at the places at which his ship called that 'he had large offers made to stay with them'. But George had his eye on bigger things and remained on board until he arrived in England in 1646.

First he became an itinerant preacher, but with the turmoil of civil war going on around him, he inevitably saw a better chance of establishing himself now that he was back in England. So he was 'called to be a preacher' in Colonel John Okey's regiment in the army of Sir Thomas Fairfax, who commanded the Parliamentary forces in the North. Okey was to rue the day that he ever set eyes on Downing.

The ambitious and ruthless young man gradually dropped his role as preacher to the army and edged his way towards the beginning of his true career. Somehow – and he seems to have covered his own tracks with consummate skill – he wormed his way into the confidence of Oliver Cromwell himself, and in 1649 became the Commonwealth's Scoutmaster General in Scotland. A less delicate title would have been Cromwell's master spy – and spying, from now on, was to be his career, and to make his fortune. At the age of about twenty-six, he was getting the very considerable sum of £365 a year, plus £4 a day to pay for his network of spies. He was already investing in property which was bringing him in some £500 a year, and as his mother could now proudly write: 'Georg is the only thrieving man of our generation.'

Downing was now very much in Cromwell's closest circle, and was with him at the Battle of Worcester in 1651. He was keeping very firm tabs on what was happening within the Army – the Council of State ordered him to 'take care that daily notice be given to the Council of what passes in the army' – and was ensuring that his grim-faced master was well informed of any signs of restiveness among the people who had put Cromwell in power.

In 1654 Downing married – and a very grand marriage it was. His progress to status and wealth was greatly helped when he married into the great family of the Howards. He had, it was recorded, 'passed through many Offices in Cromwell's Army, and at last got a very particular Credit and Confidence with him, and that under Countenace married a beautiful Lady of very noble Extraction, which was the fate of many bold Men at the presumptuous Time'. The 'beautiful Lady' was Frances Howard, descended from the fourth Duke of Norfolk who had been beheaded by Queen Elizabeth for his association with Mary Queen of Scots. Her brother was the first of three peers created by Cromwell, Viscount Morpeth, so presumably Downing met her through his political connections. His marriage to this young, well-connected, and wealthy lady was very splendid indeed; and not long afterwards he added to his glory by becoming a Member of Parliament.

Downing's inexorable advancement continued. For now began his diplomatic career, in which he rose to his greatest splendour – and sank to his lowest depths. In 1655, having been appointed secretary to Thurloe, Cromwell's Secretary of State, he was sent to Paris to protest to Louis XIV about the massacre of Protestants by the Duke of Savoy's troops. He 'embarked from Dover in a public ship, 4 August 1655', and was much flattered by the particular civility with which he was received by the immensely powerful Cardinal Mazarin. He eagerly reported back to London that he had been treated with 'great cuvility' and had been with Mazarin 'full two hours'. Mazarin's graciousness knew no bounds for later that evening the Cardinal 'send me his owne supper'. What is more, Downing got assurances about the safety of Protestants in the future and 'returned to England with great applause'.

Downing made his mark in the House of Commons, too. As a politician he was 'a very voluminous Speaker', but he was adamant in protecting British trade, and by supporting strict laws on the use of shipping for imports and exports did much to build up the British marine fleet. Once, when there was no chaplain present to say the daily prayers, the MPs asked him to lead them in prayer. But Downing – perhaps he had some sort of conscience – declined, and the House met that day without any appeal for divine guidance.

It was, almost inevitably, Downing who led the campaign in the Commons to persuade Cromwell to accept the title of King – the Protector was, in any case, already King in all but name. In a speech in January 1657 he told the House: 'I cannot propound a better expedient for the preservation of both his highness [Cromwell] and the people than by establishing the government upon the old and tried founda-

The Great Seal of the Commonwealth, 1651. It depicts Parliament in session and gives an unexaggerated impression of the size of the chamber

tion.' But Cromwell, although much tempted – he had already sat on the Coronation stone and carried the orb and sceptre in Westminster Hall – decided that this would be too much for the Army, and declined.

Downing got his reward, however, for later that same year he was sent by Cromwell to be the British Ambassador to the Hague at the princely salary of £1,000 a year. His letters of credence were written, astonishingly enough, by the great John Milton, who found himself able to describe Downing as 'a Person of eminent Quality, and after a long trial of his Fiedelity, Probity and Diligence, in several and various negotiations, well approv'd and valu'd by us. Him we have thought fitting to send to your Lordships, dignify'd with the Character of our Agent, and amply furnished with our instructions.' He was received with great ceremony in Holland, and settled down to do what he had been sent for – to spy on the Royalists, and especially on Charles II and his family and followers.

The talent for which he was most distinguished as a public minister and most valued to his own Government was his faculty of obtaining information of all that was going on around him . . . It may be said, with almost literal truth, that by his agents, correspondents, servants, and spies, he was everywhere present. Not a ship arrived or sailed from a port in Europe that he did not communicate to Cromwell her name, destination, owners, cargo, consignees, armament, and even the number and character of her crew. He watched the course of Charles Stuart and the other members of the exiled family, tracked their agents and adherents from court to court, and kept a list of their correspondents on the Continent and in England . . . ascertained and reported every journey Charles made, every interview he held with his friends, and even the places where he lodged, and the very rooms in which he slept from night to night.

Charles's sister lived in the Hague – she was married to William, Prince of Orange, and was the mother of the future William III of England. Brother and sister often met to plan his restoration, and their activities were watched eagerly by Downing. He protested to the States of Holland and sent them a copy of their Treaty with England that they were 'not to suffer any Traitor, Rebel or other person, who was declared an enemy to the *Commonwealth* of *England*, to reside or stay in their Dominions'. The States were obliged to notify the Princess that 'if her Brother were then with her or should come to her, He should forthwith depart out of their Province'.

Downing even did his best to ensure that prayers for the exiled British Royal family should cease. He complained that 'this way of praying, with its dependances, made this place a meere nursery of cavallierisme', and got an order from the States that it should be stopped. Not surprisingly, he was loathed by the English exiles. At least one attempt was made on his life, when three 'Englishmen, about ten of the clock at night, with their haire tucked up under their white caps, stood privatly at a bridg' near his house in an attempt to waylay him. But an innocent Dutchman was set upon by mistake, and Downing escaped.

Downing, though, was undismayed – and very pleased with himself for stopping prayers for Charles. 'I have by little and little extremely disturbed and spoyled their Kingdome here; and exceedingly angry they are at this last action of mine, in onteyning, that Charles Stuart should be no more prayed for here.'

Blackmail was, of course, well within Downing's scope – and if it involved a member of his own family that simply made it easier and more effective. His brother-in-law, Thomas Howard, proved to be a particularly useful victim. Downing used him ruthlessly, both to promote the Commonwealth's cause and then later, when the Royalists were gaining ground, to promote his own chances in that direction. Howard, who was an important member of Charles's circle in exile, had a rather rackety private life and, Downing confided to Thurloe, 'had a whoor in this country, with which he trusted his secret papers: these two afterwards falling out, a person in this town got all the papers from her'. Could 'a person' have been the virtuous Downing, consorting with a 'whoor'? But he begs Thurloe to keep quiet about the transaction for 'if it should be known that I have given you this account he would endeavour to have me killed'.

Cromwell died on 3 September 1658 and was succeeded by his hopelessly incompetent son Richard – Tumble Down Dick, they called him. Downing carefully read the omens for the future, and decided that the time was coming when he must do a smart, and totally unprincipled, about-turn, if he was to save his position, his increasing fortune, and quite possibly his head. So, from being a dedicated Commonwealth man and Cromwell devotee, he became an instant and overwhelmingly ardent Royalist. He had been reappointed to his post in Holland by the Rump Parliament in January 1660, which gave him the perfect

Right: Downing's diary for 19, 20, 22 September 1658, written while he was Cromwell's minister at the Hague. He records on 19 September 'the newes of the Death of His Highnes Oliver Ld Protect: of Engl: &c which happened on fryday the 13th of this month'

chance to make his peace with Charles II. Howard told him that Charles was planning to come to the Hague to visit his sister again, so Downing persuaded his brother-in-law to arrange an interview. On 5 April 1660 an 'old reverend-like man with a long beard and ordinary grey clothes' tottered in to the King's presence and fell on his knees. He whipped off his beard, and there, grovelling at the King's feet, was Cromwell's former spy-master. Downing babbled on about his wish to promote His Majesty's service, which he 'confessed he had endeavoured to obstruct, though he never had any malice to your Majesty's person or family'. It was, he explained, all his father's fault: old Emanuel had 'banished' him to New England, 'where he was brought up, and had sucked in principles that since his reason had made him see were erroneous'. On and on went Downing, promising to betray to the King all the information he had gathered together for Cromwell, 'if you would be so graciously pleased as to pardon his faults and errors'.

He could not particularise any great and notable service for the present, but in general he would from time to time do all he could. He believes he has a good interest in the Army, and that your Majesty can have no greater service done you than dividing the army's interest in their resolutions of vehemently declaring against your Majesty in particular, and in general against any government in a single person.

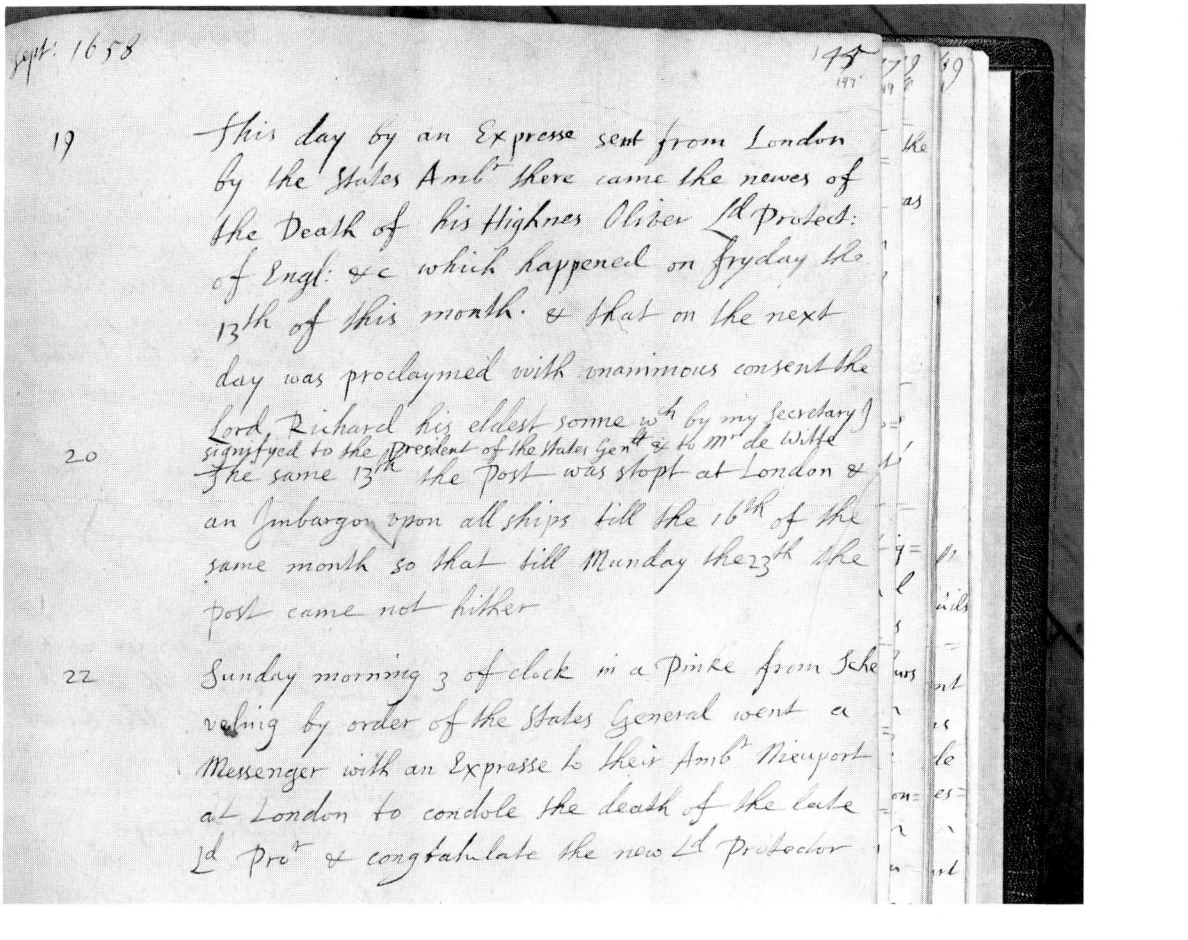
Sept: 1658 145

19 This day by an Expresse sent from London by the States Ambr there came the newes of the Death of his Highnes Oliver Ld Protect: of Engl: &c which happened on fryday the 13th of this month. & that on the next day was proclaymed with unanimous consent the Lord Richard his eldest sonne wch by my Secretary I signifyed to the President of the States Genll & to Mr de Witte

20 The same 13th the Post was stopt at London & an Imbargo upon all ships till the 16th of the same month so that till Munday the 23th the post came not hither

22 Sunday morning 3 of clock in a Pinke from Schevelnig by order of the States General went a Messenger with an Expresse to their Ambr Nieuport at London to condole the death of the late Ld Protr & congratulate the new Ld Protector

Charles needed all the help and advice he could get, from whatever quarter, and realised the usefulness of the man. Downing continued with his promises of information about the rapidly moving events in England, and bargained with Charles to keep the post of one of the Tellers of the Exchequer (it was worth £500 a year, and he had held it before going to the Hague) in exchange for spying. The King amiably and cynically agreed, and on 21 May 1660 knighted Downing. Even Charles's circle was astonished: 'They who were near the King, and knew Nothing of what had passed, wondered at as much as Strangers who had observed his former Behaviour.'

Samuel Pepys, from an original by Godfrey Kneller

With Charles back in England, Downing bustled to London after him. Samuel Pepys, who had been his clerk at the Exchequer, noted on 28 June 1660: 'To Sir G. Downing, the first visit I have made to him since he come. He is so stingy a fellow I care not for him.' It was an assessment with which Downing's mother was bitterly to agree. In her old age many years later, and back in England, she wrote complaining about his meanness. He would give her only a tiny allowance and

more . . . Georg will not hear of for me: and that it is only covetousness that maks me ask more. He last summer bought another town, near Hatley, called Clappum, cost him 13 or 14 thousand pound, and I really beleeve one of us two are indeed covetous . . . The good Lord help me to live by fayth, and not by sence, while he please to afford me a life

And George, with all his thousands, made a total contribution to his old university of Harvard of precisely £5.

Downing, with his usual eye for the main chance, now set out to catch some of the people who had been responsible for trying and condemning Charles I to death in 1649. Three of these were known to be on the Continent, and one of them was Col. John Okey in whose regiment he had been Chaplain and 'who gave him his first bread' when he had arrived back in England from America as a young man. The others were Miles Corbett and John Barkstead, and Downing bullied De Witt, the head of the Dutch Government, into allowing him to trap the three men in Delft and then spirit them back to England. He had tracked the three down in Rotterdam and Hanau in Germany through his network of spies, and he sent word to Okey that when they came to Delft 'he had no order from the king to apprehend or molest them, but that they might be as free and safe there as himself'. It was a total lie. The three men thought they had come to Delft to help set up 'severall manufactures for ye imployment of ye poor'. Instead, they found themselves trapped in a house they were staying in when, at dead of night, Downing and his armed servants rushed into the room. They were shackled and fettered, dragged off to prison, and 'cast into a nasty, moist, and dark dungeon', with 'nothing but the damp earth to repose upon'. The Delft authorities were very doubtful about the whole incident and wanted to let the three men go, but, through Downing's 'extreme officiousness', they were taken to an English frigate, the *Blackmore*, which brought them back to England. On 12 March 1662,

Colonel John Okey

Pepys noted: 'This morning we have news . . . that Sir G. Downing (like a perfidious rogue, though the action is good in the service of the king, yet he cannot with any good conscience do it) hath taken Okey, Corbet and Barkstead at Delfe in Holland and sent them home in the *Blackmore*.' Pepys saw them on their way to their execution on 19 April: '. . . I went to Aldgate; and at the Corner shop, a drapers, I stood and did see Barkstead, Okey and Corbet drawn towards the gallows at Tiburne; and there they were hanged and Quartered. They all looked very cheerful.' A pamphlet at the time bitterly attacked Downing's betrayal of Okey, 'little thinking that the New-England Tottered Chaplain whom he Cloathed and Fed at his table, and who dipped with him in his own dish, should prove like the Devil among the twelve to his Lord and Master'.

For Downing, however, his treachery led to still grander things. The King now made him a Baronet: Sir George Downing of East Hatley, Cambridgeshire, knight, where his estate was the largest in the country. At the same time 'his Majesty gave him a thousand pounds as token of his favour'. It was, of course, just the moment for Downing to raise the delicate matter of some land he had bought several years before, during Cromwell's Commonwealth. In June 1651 the Parliamentary Commissioners had sold the Crown's interest in Hampden House to two men named Robert Thorpe and William Procter. Procter died, and in November 1654, the year of his marriage, Downing bought the interest from Thorpe – he claimed later it was in settlement of a debt he was owed. With the Restoration, of course, all such transactions made by the Commonwealth Parliament of Crown land became null and void, so Downing had to act to keep hold of his property. He petitioned the King, reminding him of a royal promise made in Holland that he would 'have a care' of Downing's estates, and he was duly given a new lease on the site. He was limited in what he could build, but it goes almost without saying that he later bent the rules and considerably extended the area for development.

Downing returned from the Hague in 1665, and settled down to a busy life of politics and business manipulations. In 1666 Evelyn, the diarist, complained about him: 'One that had ben a great . . . against his Maty but now insinuated into his favour, and from a pedagogue and fanatic preacher not worth a groate has become excessive rich.' Pepys, however, seemed to have changed his mind, for when, in 1667, Downing was made Secretary to the Treasury, he wrote that he was 'mightily pleased' at the choice. Downing busied himself in Parliament, and got through an act which effectively laid down the system which still exists to this day, by which government departments had to lay estimates of their spending before Parliament. The only hitch in his smooth rise to even greater glory came in 1671 when Charles decided to send him back to Holland once more. Downing, however, was still remembered there with considerable loathing and 'when the king named him for that employment, one of the council said: "The rablle will tear him to pieces;" upon which the king smiled and said, "Well,

I will venture him." ' But the Dutch had had more than enough of the man who had boasted that he 'hath the keys taken out of De Witt's pocket when he was a-bed, and his closet opened and the papers brought to him and left in his hands for an hour'. Now they got their own back, making things so wretched for him that Downing had to scuttle back to London and abandon his post. For that act of cowardice, 'coming home in too great haste and fear, [he] is now in the prison where his master [Okey] lay that he betrayed'. The Dutch had been cruel enough to reprint his pontifications while he had been Cromwell's representative there, and they remembered him as a 'bold, rapacious, and unprincipled man, who under Cromwell had extorted by menaces considerable sums, in the form of presents, from Dutch merchants', and was so 'hateful in Holland that he fled back to England to escape the vengence of the mob'. And perhaps that extortion from the Dutch merchants explains part of the fortune that allowed him to invest in a little bit of speculative jerry-building in the heart of London.

Downing spent two months in the Tower. He found that quite enough, and settled down to a quiet life on the proceeds of his extortions and the £80,000 which he is said to have made through various favours from the King. Certainly he persuaded Charles to relax the limits which had originally been placed on the extent of the building he could do in Whitehall. By 1683 work on the houses that Churchill was later to call 'shaky and lightly built by the profiteering contractor whose name they bear' had begun. But Downing did not live to see them finished; nor did he ever live in the street that bears his name. He died in 1684, leaving, in his substantial will, the Downing Street portion of his estate to the youngest of his three sons.

If such a man needs a monument, it is there on the name plate of London's most famous street. But his evil reputation had got back to his old college at Harvard where it is recalled of that university's earliest graduate that 'his character runs low with the best historians in England; it was much lower with his countrymen in New England; and it became a proverbial expression, to say of a false man who betrayed his trust, he was an arrant George Downing'.

Top: Whitehall from the south, *c.* 1750, by Thomas Sandby
Bottom: Charles II walking in St James's Park, by Hendrick Danckerts. The tower with the turrets is the Holbein Gate, with the Tiltyard gallery in front. The Cockpit is the building with the octagonal roof and the 'house-at-the-back' is on the right. The picture hangs in the ante-room of the Cabinet Room at No. 10

Above: Sir Thomas and (*right*) Lady Knyvet, by Daniel Mytens. They lived in a house on the site of what was to become Downing Street, from where Sir Thomas was called to arrest Guy Fawkes

George Villiers, 2nd Duke of Buckingham, 1675, by Peter Lely. He lived in the house-at-the-back

Oliver Cromwell, *c.* 1653/4, by Peter Lely

Sir George Downing, who built Downing Street and gave it its name. This portrait hangs in Downing College, Cambridge, and is a copy of a portrait at Harvard University, but recent research has cast doubt on its authenticity

Top: Charles II in exile, dancing with his sister Mary at the court in the Hague, by Cornelius Janssens

Bottom: The Restoration of Charles II, 1660, by Isaac Fuller. The Royal procession passes along Whitehall, near the entrance to Downing Street

Above and left: Three portraits of Sir Robert Walpole, all hanging in No. 10. The engraving (*above*) is the first of the portraits of Prime Ministers which now line the main staircase. The half-length portrait (*top left*) is in the entrance-hall. The head and shoulders version (*left*) hangs over the Prime Minister's chair in the Cabinet Room. All are taken from the original painting by J. B. van Loo which is now in the Hermitage Museum, Leningrad

Above right: Sir Robert Walpole with his family and friends. His second wife, Maria Skerrett, is seated in the foreground beside Sir Robert; behind her are his son Horace and their illegitimate daughter Maria
Right: Catherine Shorter, Walpole's first wife, by Michael Dahl
Far right: Maria Skerrett, Walpole's mistress and second wife, by J. B. van Loo

Above: George II, by John Shackleton, *c.* 1750. This portrait now hangs in the State Dining-room at No. 10
Right: Queen Caroline of Ansbach, wife of George II, by Joseph Highmore

CHAPTER FOUR
Sir Robert Moves In

From the *London Daily Post*, 23 September 1735: 'Yesterday the Right Hon. Sir Robert Walpole with his Lady and Family, removed from their House in St James's Square, to his new House adjoining to the Treasury in St James's Park'. No. 10 Downing Street had become the Prime Minister's residence – or so it would seem from that simple announcement. The circumstances were rather different.

To begin with, No. 10 Downing Street was then No. 5 and was not renumbered until 1779. The numbering of the street was a haphazard affair – No. 1 is shown, on different plans, as being at opposite ends of the street – and houses were usually known by the name or status of their occupier. So, for many years, No. 10 was known as the First Lord of the Treasury's House. The numbers in the street eventually went up to 20 and more, but now, of course, only the three famous numbers remain – No. 10 for the Prime Minister, No. 11 for the Chancellor of the Exchequer, and No. 12 for the Government whips.

Nor, when he moved in, would Sir Robert have thought of himself as Prime Minister. It was a title which he certainly never used, and when it was used by others it was generally meant as a term of abuse. Samuel Sandys, who was later to live in No. 10 himself, and who led the attack on Walpole in the Commons that was eventually to bring about his downfall, claimed that 'according to our constitution we can have no sole and prime minister: we ought always to have several prime ministers or officers of state; every such officer has his own proper department; and no officer ought to meddle in the affairs belonging to the department of another.' There were voices in the Lords, too, who were persuaded that 'a sole or even a First Minister, is an officer unknown to the law of Britain, inconsistent with the constitution of this country, and destructive of liberty in any government whatsoever'. Walpole himself disclaimed ambitions of any such kind: 'As one of His Majesty's council I have only one voice.'

In practice, Walpole certainly was the first Head of Government, as distinct from Head of State, and so became the first person to have, and to use, the powers of Prime Minister. He was helped by the fact that the Hanoverian King George I, who succeeded Anne in 1714,

NUMB. 73.

The London Daily Post, AND GENERAL ADVERTISER.

TUESDAY, SEPTEMBER 23, 1735.

DRURY-LANE.
By His Majesty's Company of Comedians,
AT the Theatre-Royal in Drury-Lane, this Day, September 23, will be presented a Play, call'd
VENICE PRESERV'D; OR, A PLOT DISCOVER'D.
Written by Mr. Otway.
The Part of Pierre, by Mr. Mills; Jaffier, Mr. Milward; Bedamar, Mr. W. Mills; Priuli, Mr. Boman; Renault, Mr. Cibber. Belvidera, Mrs. Thurmond.
To which will be added, a Grotesque Pantomime Entertainment, call'd
COLOMBINE COURTEZAN.
Intermix'd with SONGS.
The Character of Pierot by Monf. Poitier; Harlequin, Monf. Le Brun; Colombine, Mrs. Clive; Spaniard, Mr. Salway.
Concluding with the Representation of the
RIDOTTO AL' FRESCO.
With proper Scenes, Machines, &c.
Boxes 5 s. Pit 3 s. Gallery 2 s.
By His Majesty's Command, no Persons to be admitted behind the Scenes, nor any Money to be return'd after the Curtain is drawn up.
To begin exactly at Six o'Clock.

COVENT-GARDEN.
By the Company of Comedians.
AT the Theatre-Royal in Covent-Garden, To-morrow, September 24, will be presented a Comedy, call'd
RULE A WIFE AND HAVE A WIFE.
The Part of the Copper Captain, by Mr. A. Hallam; Estifania, Mrs. Horton; Leon, Mr. Ryan; Duke, Mr. Hale; Cacafogo, Mr. Mullart; Don Juan, Mr. Marshall; Sanchio, Mr. Aston; Alonzo, Mr. Wignell. Margarita, Mrs. Buchanan; Altea, Mrs. Stevens; Old Woman, Mr. Hippisley.
To which will be added,
The NECROMANCER; OR, HARLEQUIN DOCTOR FAUSTUS.
The Part of the MILLER, by
Monf. NIVELON,

GOODMAN'S-FIELDS.
Not Acted these Four Years.
By the Company of Comedians,
AT the New Theatre in Goodman's-Fields, To-morrow, September 24, will be presented a Comedy, call'd
WOMAN IS A RIDDLE.
The Part of Courtwell, by Mr. Giffard; Aspin, Mr. Penkethman; Col. Manly, Mr. W. Giffard; Sir Amorous Vainwit, Mr. Bardin; Vulture, Mr. Lyon; Butler, Mr. Hamilton. Miranda, Mrs. Giffard; Lady Outside, Mrs. Roberts; Clarinda, Miss Hughes; Necessary, Miss Tollet; Betty, Mrs. M. Giffard.
To which will be added, a Comic Pantomime Entertainment, call'd
The CHYMICAL COUNTERFEITS: OR, HARLEQUIN WORM-DOCTOR.
The Part of Doctor Pestle, by Mr. Penkethman; his Man Mortar, Mr. Dove; Harlequin, Mr. Lun, jun. Colombine, (Doctor's Wife) Mrs. Hamilton; her Maid, Mrs. Dove; Courtezan, Mr. Lyon; Pierot, Mr. Norris; Dropsical Men, Mr. Bardin and Mr. Hamilton.
With Entertainments of Dancing.
BOXES and BALCONIES on the Stage, 4s. BOXES 3s. PIT [illegible] GALLERY 1s.
To begin exactly at Six o'Clock.

Liverpool, Sept. 19.

ARriv'd the Diligence, Bolt, from Norway; the Prince William, Hays, from Virginia.

Deal, Sept. 21. The two Men of War and Outward-bound, as in my last, remain. Since came down Mary, Kerfoot, for Oporto; Edward, Hore, for Ireland.

Gravesend, Sept. 23. Arrived John and Betty, Straham, from Ostend; Nassau, Evans, from Guinea.

LONDON.

Letters from Venice, by the Holland Mail which arriv'd yesterday, tell us, that the Barks taken from the Imperialists, upon the Adige, did not amount to above 28; that it was true, that a Convoy of Ships set out from the

Seckendorf, to go and establish themselves towards the Moselle.

It was reported at Frankfort, at the going off of the Post, that the French had passed the Rhine, under the Cannon of Philipsburg.

The Persecution against the Protestants in Hungary, which has not ceased yet, but goes on with more Rigour than ever, has obliged Emanuel Boltz (who also has been a several Protestant Courts abroad) to come hither to Petition her Majesty, for Letters of Recommendation to his Imperial Majesty, for restoring the Churches to the poor Protestants.

The said Emanuel Bol[illegible] his All, suffer'd ve[illegible] the blind Zeal of the Roman C[illegible] in u[illegible] very barbarously, so that his Health is ve[illegible] impair'd, and putting him into Prison afterwards, out of which he made his Escape.

Yesterday the Right Hon. Sir Robert Walpole, with his Lady and Family removed from their House in St. James's Square, to his new House adjoining to the Treasury in St. James's Park.

Last Sunday the Duke of Somerset set out for his Seat [illegible]worth in Sussex, with a numerous Retinue.

W[illegible] that a Treaty of Marriage is on [illegible] will soon be con[illegible] Lord Gray, Son and Heir Apparent to the Right Hon. Harry Earl of Stamford, and the Right Hon. the Lady Mary Booth, only Daughter to the Right Hon. George Earl of Warrington.

Sunday last being St. Matthew's Day, Mr. John Neale, an eminent Apothecary in St. Albans, was chosen Mayor of that Corporation for the ensuing Year. There was a grand Entertainment provided for the Corporation at the Red Lyon.

On the 15th Day of October next, the *Professors of* Medicine in the University of Edinburgh, begin *their usual* Colleges on all the Branches of Physick.

The Happy Jennet, Mac Lesh; and the Manabella, Blake, from Lisbon are arriv'd safe in the River.

The London Daily Post announces that the Walpoles have moved into No. 10

could not speak English, and so could not preside at the Cabinet meetings. George II, too, had only a limited command of the language, and so the practical decision-making, with all the subtle and complex arguments that this involved, was more and more left to Walpole as the leader of the Whig government. His Premiership is usually considered to have begun in 1721, and it ended with his downfall in 1742 – no subsequent Prime Minister has approached such a long span of years in office.

It took the British constitution 200 years to catch up with this undoubted fact of political life. The title of Prime Minister does not appear in any Act of Parliament until the Chequers Estate Act of 1917, which gave Chequers to the nation on condition that it was first offered to the Prime Minister of the day for his use. Even then the title Prime Minister appears only in a schedule of the Act, and not in the Act itself. The first Act of Parliament to contain the title in its main text was the Minister of the Crown Act of 1937.

So it was as First Lord of the Treasury that Walpole moved in to No. 10; that No. 10 is still the home of the First Lord is commemorated by the words 'First Lord of the Treasury', worn down by years of daily polishing, above the brass letter-box on the famous black-painted front door. There had, since Norman times, been a Lord High Treasurer of England who, with the Lord Chancellor and the Lord President of the Council, had been one of the great officers at the King's court. His function was the obvious one of looking after the King's – and therefore the country's – finances, and by the time Lord Burghley held the post for twenty-five years under Elizabeth I it had grown to encompass the great affairs of state, both at home and abroad. Charles II, however, decided to put the post 'into commission': that is, to take it away from one man, and give it to a group, or board. His new Treasury Commission 'would choose such persons, whether Privy Councillors or not, who might have nothing else to do, and were rough and ill-natured men, not to be moved with civilities or importunities in the payment of money'. And the man Charles selected as secretary to his new Commission was most certainly a 'rough and ill-natured man' – George Downing, who was later, no doubt, able to put money he had made in this post towards the building of the house into which Walpole now moved. But Downing did organise the Treasury into an efficient and properly run enterprise, setting the foundations, in fact, of all today's government departments.

Being First Lord of the Treasury meant, in practice, being the Chancellor of the Exchequer too; Walpole held both offices when he moved into No. 10. The Board of Treasury Commissioners still exists, although it never meets, and although the First Lord's job did not always go with the Premiership, today it invariably does – if only because a Prime Minister only gets a pension if he or she has also been First Lord. The Second Lord of the Treasury is the Chancellor of the Exchequer, and the other five members of the Treasury Board – the Junior Lords – are MPs and Government whips in the House of Commons. Their only practical connection with the Treasury nowadays is usually to sign vast cheques and other formal documents on behalf of the Government.

When the King offered his First Lord No. 10 Downing Street as a personal gift, Walpole rather surprisingly refused. The main part of the offer was, of course, the house-at-the-back – the Bothmar House – which was far larger and grander than the one in Downing Street. It was convenient, however, to knock the two together and make one much larger property, and to turn the house round, as it were, so that the front entrance, which had previously looked on to Horse Guards Parade, was now in Downing Street. In 1732, however, Walpole did accept the property, on condition that it should 'be & remain for the Use & habitation of the first Commissioner of his Majestys Treasury for the time being', and the *Gentleman's Magazine* noted: 'Thursday, 20th July, 1732. Sir *Robert Walpole* being become an Inhabitant of the Parish of St Margaret's at Westminster, by having obtain'd a Grant of Count *Bothmar's* house in St *James's*-Park . . .; chosen of the Select Vestry.' It was three years before the existing tenants in Downing Street, Mr Chicken and Mr Scroop, had been moved out, and very extensive work had been done, so that Walpole and his family could move in.

The street they were moving into was pleasant enough, but not among the grandest in London. Some years before, in 1720, it had been described as '*Downing Street*, a pretty open Place, especially at the upper End, where are four or five very large and well-built Houses, fit for a Person of Honour and Quality; each House having a pleasant Prospect into *St James's*, with a Tarras Walk.' Two years later these houses were to let. The *Daily Courant*, 26 February 1722: 'To be Lett together or apart, by Lease, from Lady Day next – Four large Houses, with Coach-houses and Stables, at the upper End of Downing-Street, Westminster, the Back fronts to St James's Park, with a large Tarras Walk before them next the Park. Enquire of Charles Downing, Esq.; in Red-Lyon Square.' Charles was George's grandson.

The street itself, both before and after Walpole's arrival, was bordering on an area that was becoming increasingly undesirable, with the stews and brothels that abounded in Westminster creeping uncomfortably near. Some of the houses in Downing Street were ordinary lodging-houses, where MPs – especially Scottish members – stayed during the short parliamentary sittings; it was conveniently near the Commons, and after a day's sitting they could go home more safely in groups, behind the flaming torches of the link boys. James Boswell was later to live there; and Tobias Smollett tried to make his living as a surgeon there. He, and the other literary men who came to the street, could have spun out their empty time by drinking in the 'King's Head' (or 'King Henry's Head') beside the Treasury Passage that leads from Horse Guards to Downing Street; or in the 'Axe and Gate' on the corner; or they, and their political neighbours, could have bought sovereign cures for sore throats:

Louis Barbay, successor to the late Mrs *Maria Wickstead*, Being the only Person that has possession of her Secret for Curing *Sore Throats* and *Wens*, though of ever so large a Size, by her infallible *Lozenges* and *Powders*, gives Notice, that they will be sent to any Part, with *Directions* how to take them. Letters directed to me, at Mr Huckabys, the Rose and Crown, the Corner of Downing Street, Westminster, (Post paid) shall be puntually answered.

If Downing Street was not particularly grand – and one must make allowances for the eighteenth-century equivalent of estate agent's jargon in the descriptions of it – No. 10 was an undoubtedly fine property. Given the contemporary climate in both personal and public morality, therefore, it seems odd that Walpole should refuse it as a personal gift and should insist that it should be vested in the Office of First Lord. He had, after all, kept his administration together by patronage and bribery of one sort or another: he effectively bribed the King and Queen by increasing their Civil List incomes very substantially; he did not hesitate to place members of his own family in sinecures; and made substantial sums of money when he held the post not only of Prime Minister but also that of Chancellor of the Exchequer.

As a master in the art of patronage, Walpole may have seen the house as one more desirable gift that he might have at his disposal, should he ever need it. He had no pressing reason, after all, to take on the house himself. He already had two houses in London – in Arlington Street and at Chelsea (he had moved into St James's Square while No. 10 was got ready for him and his family); he had a hunting lodge, complete with pack of beagles, in Richmond Park; and his large family

William Kent, the architect who carried out extensive work at Walpole's Norfolk home at Houghton and made the alterations to No. 10 between 1732 and 1735

estates, with a splendid house, at Houghton in Norfolk, which also had a pack of hounds. His real reason for accepting No. 10 only on behalf of the First Lord may well have been a smooth piece of manipulation which meant that, in effect, he got the house but the country paid for its extensive and expensive renovation. This was done by the architect William Kent, who had done even more extensive (and expensive) work on Walpole's house at Houghton, and who was then working on the new Treasury building (more or less on the sight of Henry VIII's tennis court) in Whitehall, a few yards east of No. 10.

The Office of Works kept no records of the cost of restoring No. 10. Walpole may, of course, have paid for it himself – although he was always short of money; but the cost may also have been neatly absorbed into the £20,000 spent on building the nearby Treasury during exactly the same three years the work on Downing Street took place – 1732 to 1735. The costs at the Treasury certainly rocketed during that period; they had originally been estimated at £8000, and even allowing for unforeseen expenses, the increase was spectacular.

The state certainly took on the cost of making the Downing Street garden the year after the Walpoles moved in. On 16 April 1736 the Treasury noted that 'a piece of garden ground scituate in his Majesty's park of St James's, & belonging & adjoining to the house now inhabited by the Right Honourable the Chancellor of his Majesty's Exchequer [Walpole], hath been lately made and fitted up at the Charge . . . of the Crown'. The house and garden were 'meant to be annexed & united to the Office of his Majesty's Treasury & to be & remain for the Use

& habitation of the first Commissioner of his Majesty's Treasury for the time being'. It was, of course, necessary that 'some Skilfull person should be appointed to look after . . . the said piece of ground', so the Treasury appointed Samuel Milward as gardener to No. 10 at £40 a year. He kept his job for seventeen years, and when he died in 1753 he was succeeded by a man called George Lowe.

Whoever paid for the work at No. 10, and however much it cost, it was certainly extensive. The house had been much knocked about in the years before Walpole took it over, and Mr Chicken, and his neighbour Mr Scroop, remained in parts of it until 1734. A long corridor was constructed to join the two houses – Bothmar House at the back and No. 10 at the front – thus making the Downing Street frontage the main entrance; it meant a much shorter and quicker route to the House of Commons. A maze of small staircases was removed and the present grand staircase built, to curve up through the various storeys of the house. On the second floor Lady Walpole ruled: she had her drawing-room in what is now the White Drawing-room at the west corner of the house; and the present Blue Drawing-room, which leads off it, was her dining-room. On the floor below, Sir Robert had his three official rooms. One was his parlour, where he tactfully had a portrait of George

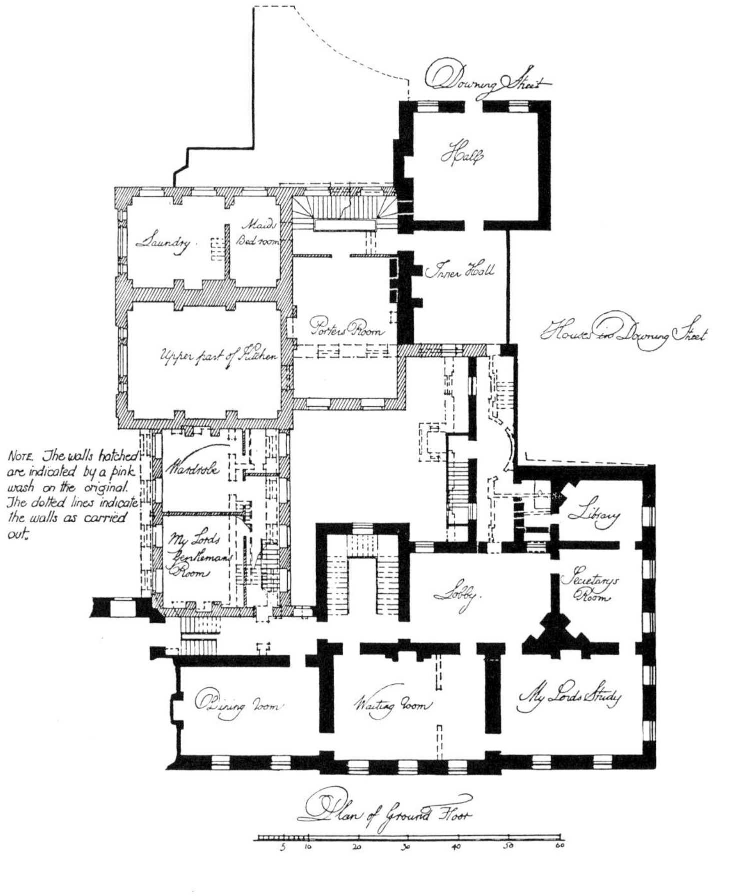

No. 10 after the alterations had been made. 'My Lord's Study' is now the Cabinet Room, the 'Waiting room' is the Principal Private Secretary's room, and the 'Dining room' is the Private Secretaries' room

II over the marble fireplace; one was the levee room, where he worked and received visitors and which eventually became today's Cabinet Room; next to it was his dressing-room, which is now used by the Parliamentary Private Secretary. On the brightly painted walls he hung his magnificent collection of pictures – one estimate in his lifetime valued them at £100,000, although a more realistic figure would probably have been about £30,000. These disappeared to the Hermitage in St Petersburg when Walpole's irresponsible grandson sold them to Catherine the Great in 1779.

Walpole was sixty, and had been Prime Minister for fourteen years, when he moved into No. 10. He was one of nineteen children, the son of a prosperous Norfolk landowner. He unexpectedly inherited the family estates after two older brothers had died, and entered Parliament first as member for Castle Rising, his father's old seat, and then, in 1702, for King's Lynn, which he represented for forty years. His rise among the Whigs was rapid and spectacular, even though he followed the ancient parliamentary tradition of making a disastrous maiden speech in the Commons. He spent an uncomfortable, although brief, spell in the Tower when he was unjustly accused of receiving money from Government contracts, but his cell became the meeting-place for the leading Whigs.

Walpole's political fortunes were made – and his personal fortune as well – out of the disaster of the South Sea Bubble of 1720. He had already served for some years as Chancellor of the Exchequer and First Lord of the Treasury, but the court intrigues of the King and his German mistresses and hangers-on, together with a group of place-seeking Whigs, had disgusted him and he had left the Government. The South Sea Company scheme was an ambitious, and wholly unworkable, plan to pay off the national debt through the giving of monopolies to the company for trade with South America. Walpole warned the Commons that it was a 'dangerous lure for decoying the unwary to their ruin by a false prospect of gain', although he bought shares himself and, either through a shrewd judgment of the market or through excellent inside knowledge, sold out at just the right moment and made a thousand per cent profit on his investment. Very few others were as lucky, and as the bubble burst and the nation was rocked by the immensity of the crash, Walpole was called back to sort out the mess. In April 1721 he again became Chancellor of the Exchequer and First Lord of the Treasury, and remained in office for over twenty years.

He was then forty-five, a loud, hearty, deep-drinking man, given to coarse jokes told in a rich Norfolk accent, who could manage the nation's finances brilliantly, but who was himself deeply in debt. He had an income from his state rents of about £8000, the money from the South Sea investment, and an income from official sources of about £9000; but he had a wife with very extravagant tastes, half a dozen legitimate and illegitimate children, and a variety of mistresses to support.

When George I died in 1727 in Germany, Walpole 'killed two horses in carrying the tidings' to the new king, George II, at Richmond. Court intrigues were still against him, but he had already charmed the new Queen Caroline by giving her excellent advice about her investments, and she used her influence with her husband to invite Walpole to continue in office. He confirmed his popularity with the Crown by increasing the King's Civil List to the enormous sum of £830,000, with £100,000 for the Queen.

Queen Caroline and Walpole got on wonderfully well. She enjoyed his coarse humour – a 'prater at Court in the style of the stews', said Swift; she did once complain that he had tapped her on the shoulder while they were in chapel, but she bustled round to Downing Street a week or so after he had moved in. The *London Daily Post*, 1 October 1735:

> This Morning about 9, the Queen, the Duke, and the Princesses, attended by the Principal Officers and Ladies of the Court, intend to come from Kensington and Breakfast with Sir Robert Walpole, at his new House near the Treasury in St James's Park. Some choice Fruits, Sweetmeats and Wines, with Tea, Chocolate etc. have been sent for the Entertainment of the Royal and Illustrious Company. Sir Robert Walpole continues to Lodge at his House at Chelsea, till the time of the Meeting of the Parliament, when he will, with his Family, remove to that in St James's Park.

Whitehall and Westminster in 1746. Downing Street is at the top of King Street

Presumably the journalist who wrote that piece did not read his own paper, for the *Daily Post* had, only a week before, announced that the Walpoles had moved into No. 10. Two days later the same paper (perhaps trying to cover its mistake) added:

When her Majesty Breakfasted with Sir Robert Walpole on Wednesday last, at his House in St James's Park, the Right Hon. the Lord Walpole, Edward Walpole, Esq., and Horatio Walpole, Esq., Sir Robert's three Sons, waited at Table on her Majesty and the Royal Family. The Earl of Grantham, by her Majesty's Orders, left a handsome Sum to be distributed among the Servants.

The meal was ceremonially served. The Queen sat at the table with Lady Walpole, and Sir Robert stood behind her chair. Sir Robert served the first course and then left; he had his breakfast in the next room with members of the Royal household. Of the three sons who served the Queen, Lord Walpole, the eldest, had been given a seat in the Lords because his father thought he himself could play a more important part in political life by staying in the Commons; and 'Horatio Walpole, Esq.,' was the brilliant wit and letter-writer, Horace Walpole.

As for Lady Walpole, she was, presumably, putting a polite face on her relationship with her husband. A woman of 'exquisite beauty and accomplished manners', Catherine Walpole brought her husband a handsome dowry of £20,000, and then settled down to squander it on extravagant jewels and high living. She spent much of her time at the house in Chelsea instead of at Downing Street, and gossip had it that Horace, who was eleven years younger than his brothers and sisters, was the result of an affair between her and George II when Prince of Wales; gossip also had it that Walpole knew but was prepared to accept it and acknowledged Horace as his son.

Catherine died in August 1737, two years after the move to Downing Street, and the Queen died in October of the same year. On her deathbed she sent for her friend and said: 'I recommend the King, my children and the Kingdom to your care.'

Walpole certainly survived the death of his first wife without too much distress, but the death of his second wife at Downing Street caused him deep and bitter sorrow. Maria Skerrett was a vivacious and wealthy woman of Irish extraction. Her father had been a prosperous merchant in Dover Street, and she became a celebrated wit and beauty. John Gay is said to have based Polly Peachum in *The Beggar's Opera* on her (Walpole himself was Macheath), and she became Walpole's mistress – certainly not his first – in 1728. By the time they were able to marry after his first wife's death – in March 1738 – she had already borne two children by him; one of them was to survive to become the housekeeper at Windsor Castle. She was brought to bed of her third child on 4 June 1739, and in the room which later was, for many years, used as the Prime Minister's bedroom, she died of a miscarriage. Walpole was heartbroken. Her death, said Horace, plunged his father into a 'deplorable and comfortless condition', although the Prime Minister was to seek comfort elsewhere in a remarkably short space of time.

Nevertheless, the zenith of Walpole's career was past. Much against his better judgment he allowed England to be dragged into the War of Jenkins' Ear against Spain in 1739: the mutilated Capt. Jenkins appeared at the Bar of the Commons, complete with the ear he said had been torn off by jeering Spaniards who had boarded his ship. 'They now ring the bells, but they will soon wring their hands,' warned the man who had tried always to follow his policy of 'let sleeping dogs lie', and as his gout and stones became increasingly painful, the meetings of his six-man Cabinet at No. 10 became increasingly noisy and abusive. He could not sleep, and as his enemies in the Commons sensed his troubles they mounted vicious campaigns against him. They forced endless divisions; insisted on sitting on Saturdays so he could not get a little relaxation with his pack of beagles at Richmond; once the Opposition even jammed dirt and sand into a keyhole of a door in the Commons to prevent the people inside getting to the division lobbies to support him.

Horace, back from the Grand Tour in October 1741, wrote from No. 10: 'I have been very near sealing this letter with black wax; Sir Robert came from Richmond on Sunday night extremely ill, and on Monday was in great danger . . . There is no news, nor a soul in town. One talks of nothing but distempers, like Sir Robert's.'

The end of Walpole's career, when it came, was on a vote dealing with a paltry matter of total unimportance: whether a petition should be allowed to be presented about possible irregularities at an election in Chippenham. His enemies used it as what amounted to a vote of confidence, and on 2 February 1742 Sir Robert was defeated by sixteen votes. He immediately resigned all his offices. George II, who had begun by loathing him, now admired Walpole deeply. When he went to St James's Palace to take his formal leave, 'the King fell on his neck, wept and kissed him, and begged to see him frequently . . .'

Walpole accepted a peerage as the Earl of Orford and a pension of £4000 a year, but stayed on at No. 10 until midsummer. Horace Walpole wrote to Horace Mann: 'I am willing to enjoy this sweet corner while I may, for we are soon to quit it.' His father after years in Downing Street was returning to a small house in Arlington Street 'opposite to where we formerly lived'. There three years later, on 17 March 1745, utterly exhausted by his tremendous life, he died. Wracked by the agony of stones, which lasted for his final six weeks, he drifted into oblivion, 'drenched with opium' to relieve his sufferings.

When Walpole fell from power, the jubilant mob burnt his effigy in the streets. But he had brought the nation through the trauma of the South Sea Bubble; had given it years of peace; and, as its Prime Minister and Chancellor of the Exchequer, had managed the nation's affairs with consummate skill and ability. His own affairs, however, were quite beyond his scope. When he died Sir Robert Walpole was £40,000 in debt.

CHAPTER FIVE

Sons-in-Law and a Satanist

After Walpole's unhappy departure from 10 Downing Street it was twenty-one years before another Prime Minister or First Lord lived there. His successors in office were men of wealth and property with their own splendid town houses, and the traditions of No. 10 had not yet had time to take root and develop. Prime Ministers clearly saw the house as just one more of the fruits of their office, which they could hand out to fellow politicians or to members of their families as they thought fit. It was to be many years, too, before the two offices of Prime Minister and First Lord of the Treasury became inseparable; by no means all the First Lords who have lived at No. 10 have also been Prime Ministers.

At first, it looked as though the house would settle down to become the home of the Chancellor of the Exchequer, the Second Lord of the Treasury; it was not until 1828 that No. 11 became his official home. After Walpole moved out, five governments came and went before a Prime Minister returned, and most of the occupants in that time were Chancellors. The first of these to live in No. 10 was the man who, ironically, reached the zenith of his career in destroying Walpole, and who then slid slowly into obscurity. Samuel Sandys was a deeply unpleasant man, though he was presumably loved by his wife and ten children – all under the age of twenty – who went with him to Downing Street. As Chancellor of the Exchequer in the new Government headed by Lord Wilmington, he moved into No. 10 in 1742, and the workmen moved in also. It was a tight squeeze for all the children, servants, clerks and men working on the 'several Repairs necessary', and the prim, mean-minded Sandys must have resented every penny it all cost him. Although a Whig, he had set himself up in opposition to Walpole, and led the campaign in Parliament against him. But after the heady heights of abusing the Prime Minister his career lost its zest and energy, and he was left as a target for abuse and hatred from Walpole's friends and family. Known as the 'Motion Maker' because he was endlessly trying to introduce a bill into the Commons to limit the number of civil and military officers in the House, he showed his consistency when the bill was finally introduced by opposing it!

Horace Walpole, not surprisingly, loathed his father's persecutor and successor at No. 10. The Sandys were eager to get into their new home and would stand no delay. In 1745 Horace recalled: 'Four years ago I was mightily at my ease in Downing Street, and then the good woman, Sandys, took my lodgings over my head, and was in such a hurry to junket her neighbours, that I had scarce time allowed me to wrap up my old china in a little hay.' And, of course, every stick the Walpoles possessed had to go with them, since No. 10 did not then, or for many years to come, have any official furniture or fittings to go with it.

As for the junketing with the neighbours, if there were any, they must have been dismal affairs. Sandys certainly added to the gaiety, or more probably the corruption, of the nation by cutting the gin tax that Walpole had introduced, but he was personally miserable and both mean-minded and mean-pocketed. Horace Walpole said 'he never laughed but once and that was when his best friend broke his thigh'. Lord Chesterfield was at his most withering about him: 'He was without any merit but the lowest species of prostitution, enjoying a considerable post got by betraying his own party, without having abilities to be of use to any other.' He was one whose 'talents were so low that nothing but servile application could preserve him from universal contempt, and who, if he persevered all his life in the interests of his country, might have had a chance of being remembered hereafter as a useful man'.

Wilmington – 'the most formal, solemn man in the world, but a great lover of debauchery' – left office as First Lord in 1743, but his Chancellor managed to hang on to No. 10 for several months after he, too, had lost office. He became Baron Sandys of Ombersley, and gathered up various sinecure posts to keep him and his large family in comfort. But his end was undignified and painful: he died in 1770 from injuries he received when his carriage overturned as it was coming down Highgate Hill.

Henry Pelham became Prime Minister and Chancellor in 1743, and held the posts until his death in 1754. Once again the Prime Minister had his own fine house, so it was a perfect opportunity for him to indulge in some blatant political corruption. The next occupant of No. 10 was the Prime Minister's nephew and son-in-law, Henry Fiennes Clinton, ninth Earl of Lincoln, who had absolutely no right whatsoever to be there, but who lived at No. 10 for eight years. He had married Pelham's daughter, Catherine, ten years before, and he settled down in No. 10 (when he was there, since he used it simply as a town house when he could get away from his country pleasures) to enjoy the fruits of a long string of sinecures. Lincoln was, among other things, Comptroller of the Customs of the Port of London; Auditor of the Exchequer; Cofferer of the Household; Lord Lieutenant of Cambridgeshire; and a Lord of the Bedchamber. None of these gave him any reason to live at No. 10, and he played no part whatever in politics. He simply had the right father-in-law.

So did his successor at No. 10, who was the husband of another of

Downing Street in 1749. No. 5, occupied by the Earl of Lincoln, was renumbered No. 10 in 1779

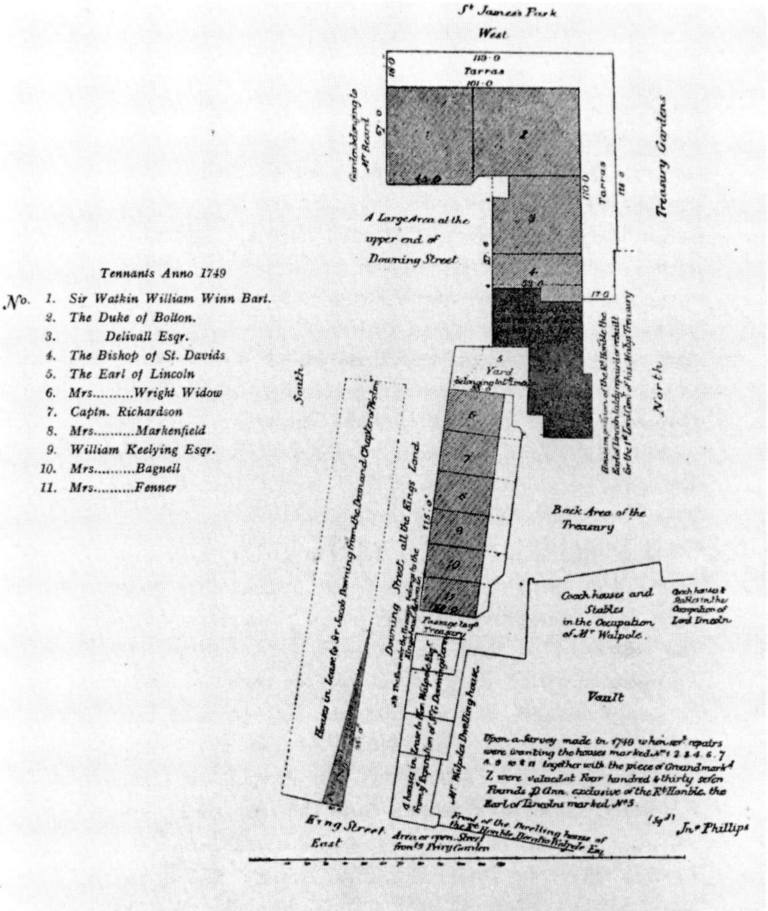

Plan of Downing Street, 1749.

Pelham's daughters. Lewis Watson had married Pelham's younger daughter, and the young couple moved in soon after their honeymoon. Unfortunately for Watson and his young bride, Pelham died the next year, and in 1754 they were firmly and crisply asked to leave since No. 10 was now wanted, once again, for the Chancellor.

The new Prime Minister was Pelham's elder brother, the Duke of Newcastle. He chose Henry Bilson-Legge as his Chancellor of the Exchequer. When Legge moved into No. 10, it was for him something of a homecoming, for he had already lived there for some years as Walpole's private secretary, and had been 'received into the family and confidence'. He had, however, been received rather too much into the confidence of Walpole's daughter, Maria, and although he was the son of an earl Walpole did not approve of the match, and Legge had to leave. But Walpole still thought highly of his abilities – 'he had very little rubbish in his head' – and Legge got himself elected to Parliament and rose steadily under the patronage of the elder Pitt. Horace Walpole, who had known him well when they were both at No. 10, deeply disliked him. He thought Legge had a 'creepy, underhand nature', and 'aspired to the lion's share by the manoeuvre of the mole'. George II shared very much the same opinion – for different reasons. Legge had, in the King's opinion, blundered over negotiations with Frederick the Great, and George agreed to his becoming Chancellor of the Exchequer only on condition that he 'should never enter his closet'.

In 1755 Legge refused to pay for mercenaries to defend the King's Hanoverian interests – 'we ought to have done buying up every man's quarrel on the continent' – and was dismissed . The rate-book for 1756 enters No. 10 Downing Street as 'E[mpty]', but not for long; the next year Legge was back in office. When he was sacked for a second time by the King in April 1757, No. 10 was again empty, but by June that year Legge was back yet again, with Pitt also reinstated as the Secretary of State. Finally, in March 1761 George III forced Legge out of No. 10 for the last time – and for much the same reason as his grandfather had done: Legge's refusal to provide British taxpayers' money to the Royal German relatives. When he went to give his seals of office to the King, Legge said: 'My future life shall testify my zeal.' The King huffily retorted: 'I am indeed glad to hear it, for nothing but your future could eradicate the ill impression that I have received of you.'

The great events of the late 1750s and early 1760s largely passed No. 10 by; neither of the Prime Ministers (the Dukes of Devonshire and Newcastle) nor the elder Pitt as Secretary of State lived there. The great decisions that led to Clive's victories in India and Wolfe's conquests in Canada and the defeat of French imperial designs were taken elsewhere. Legge had helped to pay for this tremendous empire-building by establishing a Guinea Lottery, and let it be known from No. 10 that he had bought a thousand tickets for himself. What he did not disclose was that he got rid of those tickets as quickly as possible, without losing a penny himself. It was a smart piece of cunning that would have been appreciated by the next Chancellor to live there – certainly its most extraordinary inhabitant, and one of the most extravagant – and unpleasant – men in British political history.

Sir Francis Dashwood was the quintessential eighteenth-century roué. A wealthy baronet, he inherited his title and his fortune when he was fifteen and settled down to a rakehelly life of thoroughgoing debauchery. His morals 'far exceeded in licentiousness of conduct any model exhibited since Charles II', and he had absolutely no knowledge of finance – except, presumably, gambling. He went, as a young man, on the Grand Tour, and when he came back he helped to found the Dilettanti Society of 'young noblemen or men of wealth and position, who had just come home from their travels on the continent . . . eager to be regarded as arbiters of taste and culture in their native land'. Horace Walpole said the real qualification for membership was being drunk.

Dashwood's most famous escapade was on a Good Friday in the Sistine Chapel in the Vatican. There he joined the congregation of flagellants who, as the three candles were extinguished one by one during the Good Friday ceremonies, purged their sins with their small, hired whips. Dashwood took out a full-size horsewhip from beneath his cloak and set about the penitents with a zeal that made them think the Devil himself had joined in. It was, he thought, a fine joke.

From the Dilettanti Club grew the even more notorious – and obnoxious – Hell Fire Club, of which Dashwood was the leading member. They met at the ruins of Medmenham Abbey, near Marlow, for, it was said, 'all the purposes of lasciviousness and profanity'. The twelve-strong group of Monks of Medmenham was formed of 'a number of persons, of the first distinction, in burlesque imitation of the religious societies which are instituted in other countries'. One of the members of the Dilettanti Club, Henry Vansittart, became Governor of Bengal, and from there sent home a live baboon to his brother Robert; it was promptly presented to the 'Monks' and used in their obscene ceremonies.

This was the man the new Prime Minister, Lord Bute, moved into No. 10 Downing Street as the Chancellor of the Exchequer; a man 'to whom a sum of five figures was an impenetrable secret'. The Prime Minister could probably not have done much better himself. He is said to have owed his career to a shower of rain which resulted in George II inviting him to pass the time with a hand of whist during a race meeting; there were scandals, too, about his association with George III's mother, but he kept his place in royal favour and became Prime Minister in 1762.

Dashwood's principal concern with finance was the fine that his unpleasant cronies imposed on each other if any of them happened to have some success. Gathered together in No. 10, they worked out a fine of £21 on Lord Sandwich when he was appointed Ambassador to the Congress of Aix-la-Chapelle (but only 2¾d. when he was appointed Recorder of Huntingdon); and Charles James Fox (he, together with David Garrick and Joshua Reynolds, were Dilettantis) stumped up £9 9s. 6d. when he became a Lord of the Admiralty. So busy was Dashwood about these events in his extraordinary private life that he seems to have had no time at all for his official duties; only one letter written by him survives from his eleven months at No. 10; it is seventy words long, and recommends a man as a customs officer.

At least No. 10 was not decorated with the fantastic and obscene pictures which disfigured the walls of the 'Monks'' other meeting-place, Dashwood's country house at Wycombe in Buckinghamshire, where he was painted as a sham Franciscan friar holding a goblet before a figure of the Venus de Medici and inscribed 'San Francisco de Wycombo'.

Dashwood left these ludicrous and unpleasant goings-on long enough to present just one budget to a stunned and guffawing House of Commons in 1763. He had become the MP for the ancient Cinque Port of New Romney in 1741, and the voters of that fine Kentish town – the centre of a flourishing trade in smuggled brandy and tobacco from France – must have cringed when they heard of the derision with which their Member's budget was greeted. They might, though, have approved of one of the few things it contained, a tax of 4s. on a hogshead of cider and an increased duty on wine, since that would have made their cheap smuggled spirits even more saleable and boosted their illicit trade considerably. But the whole budget statement was delivered, it was reported, in a way that was 'so confused and incapable that it was received with shouts of laughter'. Dashwood himself did have the grace to admit afterwards: 'People will point at me and cry – "There goes the worst Chancellor of the Exchequer that ever appeared." ' He was absolutely right. Citizens away from the contented smugglers in his constituency rioted at the damage his taxes would do in the cider apple-growing areas, and the House of Lords made a small piece of history by having their first division ever on a money bill – the bill, that is, which brought in the new cider tax.

Sir Francis Dashwood as a monk, kneeling in a cave worshipping a figure of Venus. An engraving after Hogarth

The Government's ineptitude over its budget, and its repressive policies, were too much for the public, and on 7 April 1763 Bute, Henry Fox, the Leader of the Commons, and Dashwood all resigned. The one saving grace in Dashwood's disreputable career was perhaps his desperate attempt to save the life of Admiral Byng who, in 1757, was shot as a scapegoat for the bungling of the war with France. He had, too, the odd distinction of being the man who, when he was sitting in the Lords as Lord Le Despencer, was the first to go to the aid of the great Chatham when he 'sank in a swoon' at the end of his last parliamentary speech.

At the time of his ignominy as Chancellor of the Exchequer, however, Dashwood was being watched with a cynical and knowing eye by one of his Downing Street neighbours: James Boswell, the biographer of Dr Johnson, wrote part of his *London Journal* (1762–3) in a house immediately opposite No. 10, and went to the House of Commons to hear the debate on Dashwood's Cider Bill. He does not mention his extraordinary neighbour in his journal, but he had chosen a 'lodging up two pairs of stairs, with the use of a handsome parlour all the afternoon', after being 'much difficulted' in finding rooms. Downing Street, he thought, was 'genteel', and he agreed to pay forty guineas a year for his rooms, but only 'for a fortnight first, by way of a trial', plus a shilling a time when he dined with his landlord and his family. Their cosy relationship did not last, however; a few months after Dashwood left Downing Street Boswell moved out too. His landlord had become 'a very rude, unmannerly fellow, in whose house no gentleman could be safe in staying'. So Boswell found himself rooms in the Temple.

He did not see – or at least did not record – the departure from No. 10 of the Monk of Medmenham, with his wife Sarah, a 'poor forlorn Presbyterian prude'. Nor did he see the arrival of the first Prime Minister to live there for over twenty years: George Grenville who, like Walpole before him, in 1763 took over the house as Chancellor of the Exchequer and First Lord of the Treasury.

Walpole addressing his Cabinet, by Joseph Goupy

Sir Francis Dashwood as a tonsured monk praying to Venus. Briefly Chancellor of the Exchequer, he was one of the 'Monks of Medmenham' and a founder of the Dilettanti Society

Above: St James's Park from the terrace of No. 10 Downing Street, *c.* 1736/40, by George Lambert. This picture is in the ante-room to the Cabinet Room
Left: Horse Guards, *c.* 1760, by John Chapman. No. 10 is the smaller of the two red-brick houses in the centre. The picture is in the entrance-hall of No.10

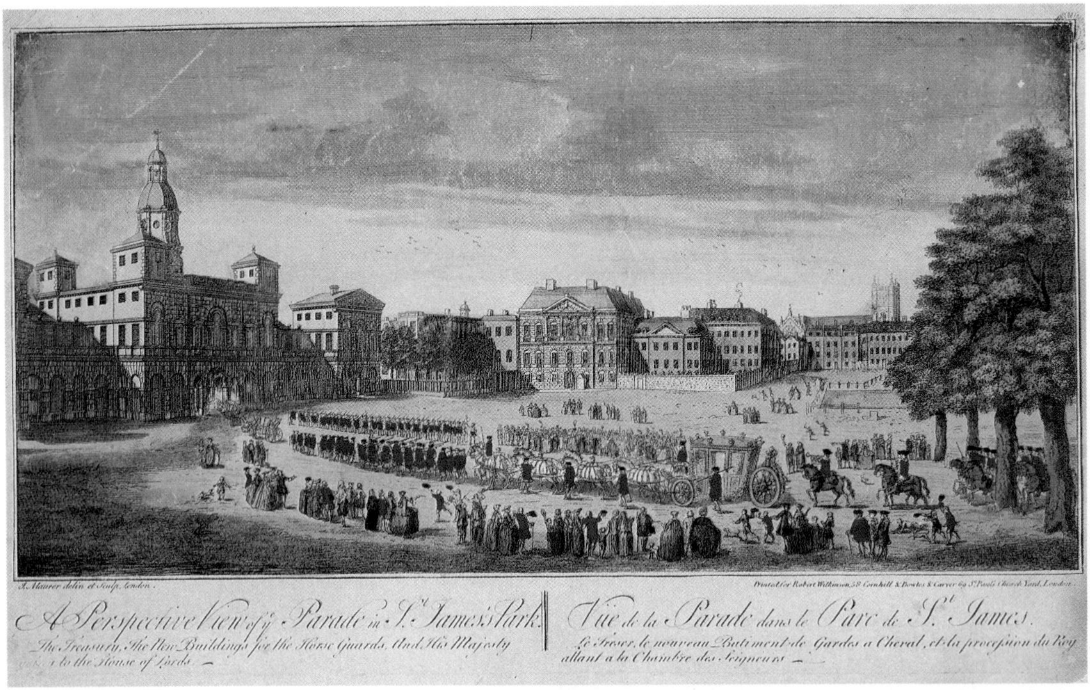
J. Maurer delin et Sculp, London.
Printed for Robert Wilkinson, 58 Cornhill & Bowles & Carver 69 St Pauls Church Yard, London.
A Perspective View of ye Parade in St James's Park.
The Treasury, The New Buildings for the Horse Guards, And His Majesty
to the House of Lords
Vüe de la Parade dans le Parc de St James.
Le Tresor, le nouveau Batiment de Gardes a Cheval, et la procession du Roy allant a la Chambre des Seigneurs

Above: View of Horse Guards, 1754, coloured engraving by J. Maurer and Robert Wilkinson

Right: William Pitt the Elder, 1st Earl of Chatham, by William Hoare, *c.* 1754. Although he did not live at No. 10, this portrait now hangs in the entrance-hall

Above: George III, by Johann Zoffany, and (*right*) Lord North, by Nathaniel Dance. Lord North was said to be the King's illegitimate half-brother

Below: Horse Guards, 1760, by Samuel Scott. The picture hangs at the top of the main staircase in No. 10

William Pitt, 1788, by Thomas Gainsborough. He moved in and out of No. 10 – 'my vast, awkward house' – three times, and died, exhausted from drink and overwork, aged 46

Right: 'Uncorking Old Sherry', by James Gillray. Pitt was a notorious toper, though of port rather than sherry

Above: Pitt's desk in the Blue Drawing-room at No. 10

'A Voluptuary', a caricature of the Prince Regent
by Gillray, 1792

CHAPTER SIX

'My Vast, Awkward House'

As Prime Ministers or, just as frequently, Chancellors of the Exchequer succeeded each other as tenants of 10 Downing Street, they and their often huge families, and their armies of servants and officials, had somehow to cope with the never-ending repairs and alterations that were going on around them. In the eighty years after Dashwood moved out, the house was constantly being repaired, shored up, modernised and extended. The bills were enormous, and the newspapers raged against the extravagance. Estimates were hopelessly wrong; everything took much longer than had been expected; workmanship was shoddy and repairs had to be made to repairs. It was all in exact anticipation of the rows that were to follow the massive modernisation of No. 10 in the 1960s.

The four men who succeeded Dashwood at No. 10 contrived, between them, to lose Britain's American colonies. Perhaps they were distracted by the crashing and banging of the workmen that went on around them; perhaps, on at least one occasion, by the crowding into the house of a troop of grenadiers sent to protect them from the mob; perhaps they were just short-sighted and incompetent.

The first of the four was George Grenville – the St Margaret's parish rate-book got his name wrong and entered him as the 'Honble George Grenwell'. He moved in in 1763, when the place was already beginning to show signs of dilapidation, in spite of the large sums spent on it only thirty years before. Horace Walpole, jealous of anyone who lived in his beloved Downing Street, said of Grenville: 'Scarce any man ever wore in his face such outward and visible marks of the hollow, cruel and rotten heart within.' He 'lost the American colonies', it was said, 'because he read the American despatches, which none of his predecessors ever did'. These despatches showed that Britain was paying out enormous sums of money in its successful defence of its North American colonies against the French, and Grenville argued that, as the colonies had also prospered through the Seven Years War, their inhabitants should contribute towards their own defence costs. The result of his logic was the Stamp Act, worked out in Downing Street amid the hammering and banging of the workmen, which enforced the purchase of British stamps on every deed, licence, newspaper, advertisement, almanac, calendar and pack of playing cards purchased in America. The Act, on which the anti-British resentment in America was bred, was passed on 22 March 1765. George III, however, was unimpressed with Grenville's policies, and bored by his pomposity. He would, he said, rather see the devil in his closet than his Prime Minister. Grenville went, and William Dowdeswell, Chancellor of the Exchequer to the new Prime Minister, the Marquis of Rockingham, moved into No. 10.

Dowdeswell was a time-server; a tedious but hard-working man for whom Horace Walpole inevitably had a bad word: 'heavy, slow, methodical without clearness, a butt for ridicule, and a stranger to men and courts'. But even Walpole could find nothing to say against his honesty and respectability; he refused any sort of preferment when, after a year, he gave up the Chancellorship. It must certainly have been a great temptation to take one or more of the available sinecures, for when Dowdeswell moved into No. 10 he took with him his wife, five sons and six daughters. Somehow they all had to cram themselves, with their servants and officials, into the house, a good half of which was taken up by offices, and which seemed to be increasingly occupied by strangers poking at the walls and knocking on the timbers. Dowdeswell, however, applied his unimaginative mind to his work, and by sheer short-sightedness made his contribution towards the growing drama of the American colonies. He did indeed, in his only budget, repeal the much-hated Stamp Act, but then undid this good with an equally offensive wrong by insisting that only the British Parliament, and not the American assemblies, had any right to impose taxation there.

In July 1766 the King called on the elder Pitt to form a new Government, and so once again No. 10 had a new tenant, and once again he was the Chancellor of the Exchequer. Charles Townshend, who had been Paymaster-General in the previous two administrations, was summoned to his new job by Pitt: 'Sir,' wrote the Prime Minister, 'You are of too great magnitude not to be in a responsible place: I intend to propose you to the King tomorrow for the Chancellor of the Exchequer, and must desire to have your answer to-night by 9 o'clock.' It meant a drastic cut in salary, but Townshend saw his chances and accepted. Horace Walpole, as ever, was waspish: 'He had almost every great talent and very little quality'; but he certainly had wit and charm, plus a large amount of heavy-handed pomposity when he thought he needed to impress.

Townshend's contribution to the American débâcle was to try to make up a shortfall in British taxation by increasing taxes in the colonies. He had been defeated in the Commons by his two predecessors at No. 10, Grenville and Dowdeswell, when they insisted on cutting the English land tax from four shillings to three shillings in the pound. To make up the difference, Townshend promptly announced import duties into America on a long list of articles – including tea.

Part of the money raised by taxing the American colonies would certainly have been spent on the massive reconstruction that Townshend now ordered at his official residence. Immediately after he moved in he put in hand what became known as The Great Repair. On 12 August 1766, ten days after his appointment, the Treasury Lords were sent a note

> . . . by the desire of the Rt Honourable the Chancellor of the Exchequer. We have caused the House in Downing Street belonging to the Treasury to be surveyed, & find the Walls of the old part of the said House next the street to be much decayed, the Floors & Chimneys much sunk from the levell & no party Wall between the House adjoyning on the Westside.
>
> We are of opinion that to repair the present Walls, Chimneys & Floors next the street will not be for His Majesty's service: We have therefore made a plan & Estimate for taking down the Front next the street & also the East Flank Wall of the Hall, to build a party Wall on the Westside to prevent the danger of Fire, to repair the remaining part of the Old Building & to Erect an additional Building adjoining thereto. All which Works besides employing such of the Old Materials that are sound & good will amount to the sum of Nine hundred & Fifty pounds.

It was a pious hope, and one that was to be utterly dashed. In the end the Great Repair went on for at least eight years and cost more than ten times that estimate.

Most of this work was to be done to Downing's rickety building facing on to Downing Street, and it was this Great Repair that gave the house he had built many of the features which are so lovingly preserved today. It was now that No. 10 acquired its famous oak front door, with its black-painted lion's-head knocker and brass letter-box, and its semi-circular fanlight above it. The elegant wrought-iron archway, surmounted by a lantern, was placed in front of the door, and the façade of the house changed to its present appearance. Inside, the entrance hall was laid with a chequered pattern of black and white marble squares which it still keeps today.

Townshend ploughed on with his disastrous American policy as the workmen hammered and banged away around him. He still managed to lead a life of some luxury among all the chaos. Once he was called unexpectedly from No. 10 to make a speech in the Commons after he had been lunching at home rather too well. His speech – the 'Champagne Speech' – was rambling and incoherent. Walpole thoroughly enjoyed himself: 'To the purpose of the question he said not a word . . . It was Garrick writing and acting extempore scenes of Congreve.'

But the high living, and possibly epilepsy, took their toll. On 4 September, after living in Downing Street for thirteen months, Townshend died there 'of a putrid fever'. The *London Chronicle* noted: 'To-morrow the remains of the Right Hon. Charles Townshend, Esq., will be carried from his house in Downing-street, Westminster, in order to be interred in the family vault at Raynham in Norfolk.'

Three months later Lord North, the new Chancellor of the Exchequer, moved into No. 10, and the final part of the American drama began. The *London Chronicle* noted his move in December 1767: 'His Lordship is going to remove from his late house near the Pay Office, Whitehall, to the house which was inhabited by the late Right Hon.

Charles Townshend Esq.' The workmen were still there as Lord North and his family settled in for their fifteen-year residence, and they were to be filling the place with dust and confusion during much of that time.

Lord North was thirty-five when he moved into No. 10, and took with him the rumour that he was the King's illegitimate half-brother by the King's late father, the Prince of Wales. King and Privy Councillor certainly looked very much alike, and Walpole, in his usual way, said 'he had two large prominent eyes that rolled about to no purpose', with 'a wide mouth, thick lips and inflated visage' which gave him 'the air of a blind trumpeter'. He was, indeed, half-blind and was said to have too large a tongue for the size of his mouth.

When the Cabinet met at No. 10 on 1 May 1769, under the premiership of the Duke of Grafton who had succeeded Pitt the previous year, it was decided, by a majority of one vote, to repeal all the import duties imposed in America, except the 3d. a pound on tea. This was kept to remind the colonials that the Westminster Parliament still retained its power over their affairs. Eighteen months later Grafton resigned, and North now became the third Prime Minister to live at No. 10. He had, besides the problems of the American colonies, to deal with a great outcry that blew up suddenly over the British possession of the Falkland Islands. Two hundred years before that other great Falklands drama kept No. 10 in a frenzy of dramatic activity, North had to face Opposition fury when he did nothing about the Spanish seizure of the islands. When he finally acted, carrying out a major review of Britain's naval strength and increasing taxes to pay for improvements, the situation over the Falklands was, he said, of 'precarious peace, of too probable war'. Luckily he was wrong, and the islands were returned to Britain without any bloodshed.

But there was to be bitter bloodshed over the American colonies. It took two months for news of the demonstration by colonists in Boston Harbour, the 'Boston Tea Party', to reach North at No. 10. Two months after that, in April 1774, Parliament revoked the charter of the colony of Massachusetts, and the port of Boston was closed until the dumped tea was paid for, and until 'it should appear to the King in Council that the people of Boston are submissive to law and good order'. All Americans arrested for sedition were to be brought to England for trial.

The first shots in the American War of Independence, which was to last for over six years, were fired at Lexington on 19 April 1775 North was at No. 10 when, on Sunday, 25 November 1781, he heard that Cornwallis had surrendered, with 7000 men, at Yorktown five weeks earlier. The message had been sent from Falmouth, via the semaphore which whirled its arms above the Admiralty in Whitehall, to Lord George Germain's house in Pall Mall. He rushed to No. 10 to tell North. The Prime Minister took the news 'as he would have taken a ball in his breast': Germain reported that North 'opened his arms, exclaiming wildly, as he passed up and down the apartment during a few minutes,

Cornwallis and the British surrender their arms to Washington after the battle of Yorktown, 1781. An engraving after J. F. Renault

"Oh God! it is all over." ' He repeated the words 'many times under emotions of the deepest consternation and distress'.

Yet North had remained unemotionally cool and calm when, a year earlier, the threat had been not across the Atlantic, but upon his own doorstep at No. 10. On 7 June 1780 London was literally alight with anti-Popery. North had made some concessions to Catholics in Britain, and had thus raised the fury of the Protestant faction, and especially of the mad Lord George Gordon and his Protestant Association. As Lord George's mob followed him through the streets of London, it set fire to buildings and destroyed those it could not burn. In due course the mob marched on Downing Street, where North was having dinner with friends. Sir John Macpherson, later Governor-General of India, was one of the guests:

> We sat down at table, and dinner had scarcely been removed, when Downing Square, through which there is no outlet, became thronged with people, who manifested a disposition, or rather a determination, to proceed to acts of outrage . . . Mr Brummell, Lord North's private secretary, who lived likewise in the same street, was in attendance, but did not make one of the company. [Mr Brummell was the father of Beau Brummell, who was precisely two years old on that day.] With his habitual good humour, the Prime Minister asked what was being done to defend No. 10. There were, he was told, 'twenty or more grenadiers, well armed, stationed above stairs . . . ready on the first order to fire on the mob'. He gave instructions that 'two or three persons' should be sent out to the mob to warn them there were troops in the house ready to fire if there was 'any outrage'.
>
> The populace continued to fill the little square, and became very noisy, but they never

The Gordon Riots, 1780. The mob set fire to buildings before marching to Downing Street

attempted to force the street door . . . By degrees, as the evening advanced, the people . . . began to cool and afterwards gradually to disperse without further effort. We then sat down again quietly at the table and finished our wine.

Night was coming on [continued Sir John], and the capital presenting a scene of tumult and conflagration in many quarters, Lord North, accompanied by us all, mounted to the top of the house, where we beheld London blazing in seven places, and could hear the platoons firing regularly in several directions.

The mob did not get near the Prime Minister on that occasion. He had once come near to death when his coach was attacked by a furious crowd in New Palace Yard at the Houses of Parliament. The mob had been out in support of John Wilkes and his demands for freedom of the press. They had surrounded North's coach and smashed it to matchwood. North was beaten about the head by the truncheons that the rioters had stolen from the constables, and he had only just escaped with his life into Westminster Hall. Yet he was the same Prime Minister at whose doorway in Downing Street beggars used to huddle for their handouts of charity. On Sunday mornings he would appear on the doorstep and give food and quarter-guineas to twenty poor people who had gathered there.

On other days North would carefully avoid the loiterers round his front door, for they would quite probably be his creditors trying, yet again, to get paid. As his political problems increased, so did his domes-

'The Horse of America throwing its Master.' A contemporary caricature of George III

tic worries as his debts mounted higher and higher. He found it difficult to sleep in his room at No. 10, and it came as a relief when, in March 1782, he was able to return to dinner in Downing Street having announced his resignation in the Commons. He had, as so often in the past, to pick his way round the builders' equipment which once again littered No. 10. A Memorial of the Board of Works, dated 12 June 1781, reported on:

> the dangerous state of the old part of the House, inhabited by the Chancellor of the Exchequer. That it is their opinion no time shall be lost in taking down the said building; and they have therefore made Plans & Estimates of the expence of rebuilding the same, which will amount to £5500.

Once again, the estimates were hopelessly low.

North's successor at No. 10, William Pitt, moved in and out of the house three times during his dazzling career. He went there first as the 23-year-old Chancellor of the Exchequer in Lord Shelburne's ministry in 1782, and although his stay was only a matter of months, he acquired a taste for the house. Downing Street was, he wrote to his mother, 'the best summer town house possible'. By July, he wrote that he expected to be 'comfortably settled in the course of this week in a *part* of my vast, awkward house'. It was always vast for the unmarried Pitt; and he could settle only in part of it because the builders were still in.

The estimates for work in the previous year had already gone completely awry. In March 1782 the Board of Works reported that 'the repairs, Alterations & Additions at the Chancellor of the Exchequer's House will amount to the sum of £5580, *exclusive of the sum for which they already have His Majesty's Warrant*'. The cost, in fact, amounted to £11,078, more than double the amount originally estimated, and ten times the amount specified when work had begun in 1766. No wonder the newspapers fulminated. As the money kept on pouring out, the *Morning Herald* thundered: 'Downing-street House – Five hundred pounds per annum preceeding the great repair, and eleven thousand pounds the great repair itself! So much has this extraordinary edifice cost the country! – For one moiety of which sum a much better dwelling might have been purchased, even supposing government to have been the purchaser.'

Still, the house was in good enough repair for the Duke of Portland, during his brief ministry, to 'give a grand turtle-feast to several of the Nobility, at his house in Downing-street', in August 1783, but later that month the *Morning Herald* announced: 'The Duke of Portland is removed to Burlington-House, where his Grace will reside while his house in Downing-street is repairing.' The 'repairing' included the extension of the Cabinet Room by taking in part of the secretaries' room next door, and putting in the two pairs of columns which support the floor above; and the extension of the big drawing-room, again with pillars at one end.

Pitt, in his brief first stay at No. 10, counted the cost of all the work that was going on there. 'The alterations that had cost £10,000 he stated to consist of a new kitchen and offices, extremely convenient, with several comfortable lodging rooms; and he observed, that a great part of the cost, he had understood, was occasioned by the foundations of the house proving bad.' Those bad foundations were to occasion a great part of the cost of modern repairs, too.

Altogether Pitt lived for twenty years in Downing Street. He was there as Prime Minister (he was twenty-four when he first took office) from 1783 to 1801, and again from 1803 to 1804. And as the work in his official house went on the accounts were kept down to the last farthing: 'Mason, £1531 0s. $7\frac{3}{4}$d.; Joiner, £1292 8s. $3\frac{1}{2}$d.; Painter, £26 7s. $6\frac{3}{4}$d.' That particular bill, in 1784, came to a grand total of £11,078 3s. 6d.

As he struggled with the nation's affairs so forcefully, Pitt was incapable of dealing with his own domestic economy. At first his youngest sister, Lady Harriet Pitt, lived with him and managed his household, but she married two years after he became Prime Minister, and while he was busy establishing the greatest Empire the world had ever seen, and bringing order and vision to political and public life at home, his servants were cheating him and the tradesmen were once again on the doorstep of No. 10. As the empty port-wine bottles piled up – Pitt had been recommended port as a stimulant by his doctor as a young man, and had taken to his medicine with ever-increasing enthusiasm – the creditors became more and more pressing.

It was commonly asserted that the Collector of Taxes found more difficulty in levying them from the Chancellor of the Exchequer, than from almost any other inhabitant of Westminster. Even Tradesmen's Bills, particularly those of Coachmakers, were said to be frequently paid, not in Money, but by ordering new Articles, and thus augmenting the Pressure of the Evil itself.

Pitt had twenty-seven servants with him at No. 10, with wages amounting to over £321 a year. The man who, when William Wilberforce came frequently to see him, planned the emancipation of slaves, was himself a slave to port and to debt. By the turn of the century he owed over £45,000 but still entertained in a lavish fashion: for one dinner, the fishmonger alone supplied pea fowl, a hare, snipe, larks, larded capons, roasted pheasant and much more.

The hopes of fifteen years of peace, which Pitt had forecast in 1792, were wrecked a year later when France declared war on England and Holland. The promised peace became twenty years of war in which, said Lord Macaulay, 'great as Pitt's abilities were, his military administration was that of a driveller'. As the war dragged on the mob was out again in Downing Street, and the Volunteers and Horse Guards were there to protect his house. The rioters threw stones at his windows but, Pitt told his mother, 'it hardly merited a notice in the newspapers'.

The Prime Minister's increasingly difficult and debt-ridden life nearly came to an abrupt end on 29 May 1798 when he fought a duel. He had been challenged by George Tierney, a Whig MP, who claimed that Pitt had insulted him during a debate in the House. The two men met on Putney Heath, fired two shots at each other, missing on each occasion, and, on the insistence of their seconds, agreed that honour had been satisfied. The Speaker of the Commons, Henry Addington, the son of the obliging doctor who had prescribed medicinal port for young Pitt, watched the affair, and then asked Pitt back to Speaker's House for dinner.

It would, at least, have been a well-cooked and well-organised meal away from Pitt's chaotic household. There had been strong rumours that he would marry Eleanor Eden, the daughter of his Postmaster-General, Lord Auckland, and they were known to be much in love. Pitt, however, decided that the burden of his debts was too great. He explained his decision to Auckland in a 'most private letter', and said that whoever had the 'good fortune to be united to her is destined to more than his share of human happiness'.

As a man of peace, Pitt had tried desperately to end the war with France and also to settle the interminable Irish problems by the Act of Union and with measures to relax the penal laws against Catholics. The King, drifting in and out of madness, objected violently to any measures which would make Catholics acceptable in public life. Pitt's plans were betrayed to the King by his own Cabinet members, and his ministry came to an end at the beginning of 1801.

The new tenant of No. 10 was the man who had watched Pitt's duel and then invited him to dinner – his friend since boyhood, Henry Addington. He moved in with his wife, son and four daughters, an unworthy successor but acceptable to the King. He managed to patch up a temporary peace with France, while Pitt, who, as Lord Warden of the Cinque Ports, had moved to Walmer Castle in Kent, peered across the Channel through his telescope, and marched a troop of volunteers up and down on the top of the white cliffs. The friendship between the two men cooled – they wrote to each other rarely now, and each time as 'Dear Sir' – and the country hoped that 'the peace which everybody is glad of and nobody is proud of' would last. It did not. Napoleon was on the march again by October 1802, eight months after Parliament had agreed to Addington's peace terms, and by May 1803 England was once more at war. The country wanted Pitt again, and in May 1804 he was back in No. 10, with his brilliant and vivacious niece Lady Hester Stanhope as his hostess.

Hester Stanhope was the daughter of an eccentric Earl who had married Pitt's sister. As a supporter of the French Revolution, he dropped his title and called himself 'Citizen Stanhope'. Hester was lively, talkative, tactless and highly intelligent – a forerunner of the equally brilliant Margot Asquith who was to be the hostess at No. 10 over 100 years later. The bright young things flocked to the house; the sedate Whig ladies kept away. Hester tried to put Pitt's house literally in order, and stop such abuses as the servants' weekly order of nine hundredweight of meat, but her own love of entertaining simply meant

Lady Hester Stanhope. She later went to live on Mount Lebanon in Syria and adopted local dress

that the bills mounted even higher. As for Pitt, he enjoyed her being there. Once, when some young relatives were visiting, they were all romping together in Pitt's office, with the Prime Minister's face smeared with burnt cork. Suddenly Lord Castlereagh and Lord Liverpool were announced. Pitt wiped his face clean, hushed the children, received the visitors with due dignity, and then, as soon as they were gone, got on with the riotous game at full pelt.

But this was an all-too-brief relaxation from his enormous burden of work. Lady Hester complained at the nation's ungratefulness for all he did for the people. Up at eight, endless meetings and interviews, a hurried meal of a mutton chop, and then to the Commons until the early hours of the morning. 'It was enough to kill a man – it was murder.' He struggled to lead a weak cabinet and to contain the French ambitions, and got at least some justification of his efforts when news came of the victory at Trafalgar. But even that was saddened by the accompanying news of the death there of Nelson, and he spent a sleepless night pacing his bedroom after he heard the news. His medicinal bottles of port had now gone up to four a day; he sometimes went drunk to the House, and was once sick outside the door behind the Speaker's chair, which he held open with his foot so he could follow the debate.

It was, of course, too much for any man. The crowds cheered him but that could not regain his health. Pitt went to Bath for the waters, but while he was there news came of Napoleon's victory over the Austrians and Russians at Austerlitz. Pitt decided to return to London, but got only as far as his house at Putney. He had already arranged a dinner at No. 10 on 19 January 1806, in honour of the Queen's birthday, and sent Hester to Downing Street to make sure it went ahead as planned. It was a melancholy meal, with the guests aware that their host was near death. William Pitt died at Putney in the early hours of the morning of 23 January, aged forty-six. His last words were: 'O my country! How I love my country!' When it was all over, his brother James got into one of the carriages that had been waiting at the house, and took Pitt's keys to No. 10. There he 'sealed up everything' and locked Mr Pitt's front door for the last time.

CHAPTER SEVEN

Ministers and Murder

For the first seventy years after Pitt's death, the keys of 10 Downing Street were held, with few exceptions, by political and historical non-entities. It was to be another 100 years before the immutable tradition of Prime Ministers always living in the house was finally established. In the years between, Wellington moved in for a short time while his magnificent home Apsley House – No. 1, London – was got ready for him; Canning spent his last months, in great pain, at No. 10; Lord Grey plotted the Great Reform Bill there; two of its tenants gained a melancholy posterity as the victims of mad assassins; another did wonders for the nation's heritage while wrecking the nation's economy; but eventually No. 10 became a rookery for quill-pushing clerks, while the state rooms – and the Cabinet Room itself – stood empty and gathered dust, and Downing Street grew shoddy and undesirable as a London address.

Pitt's immediate successor at No. 10 was William Wyndham Grenville, Lord Grenville, First Lord of the Treasury. He already knew the house, for his father had been Prime Minister in 1763 when he was four. They are the only father and son both to have been tenants of No. 10; although both Pitts were Prime Minister, the elder Pitt did not live in Downing Street.

The *Morning Herald*, 14 February 1806: 'Lord and Lady Grenville visited yesterday Mr Pitt's late house, in Downing-street. His Lordship gave orders that everything might be ready for the reception of his family by next Monday week.' It was a pious hope. By 6 March it was announced that 'Lord Grenville will not remove to Downing-street till after Easter'. The ravages of Pitt's bachelor years there were obviously displeasing to Lady Grenville. On 17 March there was a further announcement: 'The Board of Works have promised that Lord Grenville's house in Downing-street, shall be ready for his Lordship's reception in a month. Lady Grenville attends daily at the house to inspect repairs.' It was not until 24 April 1806 that the papers announced that 'Lord Grenville removed yesterday to his new residence in Downing-street'.

Even then the workmen had by no means finished. On 18 April

Father and son at No. 10. George Grenville (*left*) and William Wyndham Grenville, Lord Grenville, by John Hoppner, *c.* 1800

Charles Alexander Craig, the foreman who had been in charge of repairs twenty years before, reported that 'owing to the bad state of repair of the House of the First Lord of the Treasury the necessary work to be done there will amount to about £2200 and certainly cannot be completed in less than a fortnight'. It would certainly have taken a great deal more than a fortnight to complete such expensive repairs, while Craig would have had plenty of time to contemplate the fact that a good deal of the money was being spent on repairing the repairs that he had made when he had worked on the house before.

Grenville formed his 'Ministry of All the Talents' – Addington, once of No. 10, was Lord Privy Seal and Fox was Foreign Secretary – but his 'cold and unsympathetic manner' made him unpopular. Lady Hester Stanhope, hardly unbiased, said that, with Pitt to guide him in his career, Grenville 'did pretty well; but as soon as Mr Pitt was dead, he sank into obscurity'. Sheridan, who was in Grenville's ministry, said of him: 'I have known many men knock their heads against a wall, but I never before heard of a man collecting bricks and building a wall for the express purpose of knocking his brains out against it.' Grenville did, however, have one great achievement: he carried the resolution in Parliament for the abolition of the slave trade. He tried, too, to ease the lot of Catholics with a bill to allow them to serve in the armed forces, but George III was still passionately against any such thing – Catholic emancipation had been a cause of his earlier attacks of madness – and the bill was dropped. However, Grenville's opinions remained firmly the same, and the King dismissed him in March 1807. He was able to stay on at No. 10 for a couple of months, but the *Morning Chronicle* for 7 May 1807 reported: 'Lord Grenville will remove today from Downing-street to his house at Dropmore.'

The ancient Duke of Portland now tottered back into office and into No. 10. He had been Prime Minister briefly in 1783, and now, at seventy, he told the King, 'I feel conscious that my time of life, my infirmities, and my want of abilities, are not calculated for so high a trust.' He was absolutely right. Lord Malmesbury recalled later: 'I have often been with him when I thought he would have died in his chair, and his powers of attention were so weakened that he could neither read a book, nor listen for a while, without becoming drowsy and falling asleep.' They woke him up long enough to get him out of Downing Street back to his much more splendid town house, Burlington House in Piccadilly, and although he remained Prime Minister until 1809, it was his Chancellor of the Exchequer, Spencer Perceval, who moved into No. 10 and who ran the country.

Spencer Perceval moved in on 19 October 1807. The *Morning Chronicle* for 20 October reported: 'The Right Honourable the Chancellor of the Exchequer has entered into possession of the house which has for many years been occupied by the Prime Minister of England. He slept in it last night for the first time.' He slept in it for the last time on the night of 10 May 1812. The next day he was murdered.

Spencer Perceval was one of those politicians different people seemed to see in very different lights. He was known derisively as 'Little P', and was described by a fellow lawyer as a man with 'very little learning, of a conversation barren of instruction, and with strong and invincible prejudices,' including prejudices against Catholic emancipation. However, in his private life – and he had twelve children, several born while he was in No. 10 – it was said that no man was 'more generous, more kind, or more friendly than he was', and there was never a more 'affectionate husband or a more tender parent'.

Perceval came from a good family, but as a younger son was not well off. He married, much against her father's wishes, Jane, the daughter of Sir Thomas Spencer-Wilson, and she came to her wedding 'only dressed in her riding habit'. They lived at first in rooms above a carpet shop in Bedford Row, so by the time her husband had risen to the eminence of No. 10 Jane knew how to be a careful housekeeper. Perceval, likewise, was careful with the nation's finances, supplying the money for Wellington's Peninsular campaigns against Napoleon. Years later, Wellington wrote of him that 'a more honest, zealous and able Minister never served the King'. And the King himself approved of Perceval. When he refused one of the sinecures offered him, the King wrote that he could not 'in sufficient terms, express his sense of the liberality and public spirit' Perceval had shown by such self-denial.

By 1810, however, the King had become hopelessly mad, and Perceval – he had become Prime Minister on Portland's death the year before – had the difficult job of persuading the Prince of Wales to accept the Government's restrictive terms for setting up the Regency. The Prince and his brothers fumed, but eventually gave in, and the Regency Bill was passed in February 1811. Thomas Creevey, diarist, gossip and Member for Thetford, who had taken over from Horace Walpole as the waspish critic of events at No. 10, thought Perceval was betraying his cause when he later invited 'Prinny' to dinner in Downing Street. Creevey had, he wrote to his wife, seen 'four man cooks and twice as many maids preparing dinner for the Prince of Wales and Regent' in the kitchen of No. 10. 'By God!' he exploded, 'this is too much.'

Perceval deserved the light relief of a good dinner with the Prince Regent, for his troubles as Prime Minister were formidable. As well as the war in Europe, war again broke out between Britain and America, cutting the supply of cotton to the Lancashire mills. Industrial unrest grew, and soldiers were called out to quell the rioters. On 11 May 1812 Perceval was asked to go to a Commons committee that was hearing evidence about the problems of trade from a Staffordshire potter. As he arrived in the lobby of the House – the old lobby, that is, before the present Houses of Parliament were built – a man stepped forward and, with one bullet, shot him dead. Perceval died almost immediately; his last words were said to have been 'Oh, I am murdered' – and in the ensuing panic the murderer, who immediately admitted what he had done – 'I am that unfortunate man' – was grabbed and instantly hauled before the appalled House. He was packed off for trial and hanged within seven days.

The assassin turned out to be John Bellingham, the son of a Huntingdon land surveyor who had died insane. John had tried his luck in Russia as a merchant, and had been imprisoned in Archangel for five years for debt; as a result he became obsessed with Perceval's failure to get him released. When he eventually returned to England, he went to the Commons with two loaded pistols to kill the object of his obsessive resentment; in the event he had to use only one of them.

Perceval's body was taken back from the Commons to No. 10 to his grieving widow and children. From there, five days later, it went in solemn procession to the family vault at Charlton, in Kent. He was fifty. The nation had begun to see him as a great Prime Minister; the Bishop of Peterborough said he had 'trodden in the steps of the immortal Pitt', and in gratitude the Government gave his widow a grant of £50,000 and an annuity of £2000.

Perceval's successor at No. 10 was one of its longest residents – and one of its most obscure. Nicholas Vansittart lived in Downing Street as Chancellor of the Exchequer for eleven years, and made no impression whatsoever on either the house or history. He was the son of Henry Vansittart, that governor of Bengal who had sent to his brother Robert the live baboon that Francis Dashwood had used in his vicious ceremonies; but no son could have been less like his father or his uncle and their Dilettanti friends. He was a widower who never remarried, and his thoughts were very much on the higher things in life – and rather less than they should have been on the nation's finances. In one of his many budgets, which bored the house stiff with their turgid waffling, Vansittart scrapped Perceval's plans to tax breweries, and taxed instead carriages, horses, dogs and male servants. His financial schemes sounded very profound until they were worked out, and were then, all too often, found to be nonsense. The Prime Minister, Lord Liverpool, lived in his splendid town house in Whitehall, and Vansittart lived out his lonely life at No. 10. He did, however, enjoy one moment of historic excitement there. He had become much involved with the great Rothschild banking family, and used the firm's immense continental network to keep in touch with events. So it was that one evening Nathan Rothschild hurried to No. 10 with the first news of Wellington's victory over Napoleon at Waterloo.

Nicholas Vansittart, Baron Bexley, by William Owen, 1815

The war, however victorious, had to be paid for, and the Treasury's problems grew deeper and deeper. Vansittart tried increasingly ridiculous schemes to find the money; one of them, which involved the farming out of the payment of pensions to private contractors, was called the 'most curious specimen of the most ruinous species of borrowing that the wit of man could devise', and there were riots as the taxes bit deeper and deeper into the thin pockets of the hard-pressed workers. When Vansittart, in his enthusiasm to improve the nation's morals and mind, went to divine service at the Millbank Penitentiary, the women prisoners pelted him with stale bread.

The Prime Minister, too, had had enough of his Chancellor. In 1823 Lord Liverpool arranged for the King, now George IV, to give Vansittart a peerage, and the King wrote from the Brighton Pavilion that he was 'fully sensible of the value of his past services, and the high estimation in which I hold his private character'. Certainly no one could have doubted that royal reference to Vansittart's character. When he gave up office, this son of a founding member of the Hell Fire Club became President of the British and Foreign Bible Mission, and a leading light in the Church Missionary Society and the Prayer Book and Homily societies.

Prosperity Robinson – Frederick John Robinson, Chancellor of the Exchequer – who was the next tenant of No. 10 was a very different kettle of political fish. A man of the arts, a man of taste and a man of discrimination, he had built up a considerable collection of art before he became Chancellor of the Exchequer, but after he had introduced a bill against the importation of corn – so keeping up its price – the mob had burst into his house in Burlington Street and ransacked it. He took what was left when he moved, eight years later, to Downing Street.

Robinson was a fat, amiable man, with a taste for telling good dinner-table stories. Once he told a string of stories to his companion at table about the ugliness of Lord North's daughters; his companion was unamused – she was one of those daughters. He was known as the 'duke of fuss and bustle', and was immensely popular when, in his first budget, he cut window tax by half. He had a surplus of seven million pounds to play with in this first budget, and as he swung his axe at tax after tax, he was greeted with 'demonstrations of applause more loud and more general than perhaps ever before greeted the opening of

THE ASSASSINATION OF THE RIGHT HON.BLE SPENCER PERCEVAL CHANCELLOR OF THE EXCHEQUER
was murder'd by a pistol shot in the lobby of the House of Commons by an assassin John Bellingham a Merchant of Liverpool on Mondy Evening May the 11th 1812. Bellingham was Executed May the 18th at the drop in the Old
Published May 21 1812 by G. Thompson N.º 43 Long Lane West Smithfield.

The assassination of Spencer Perceval, 11 May 1812. He was murdered in the House of Commons and his body taken home to his wife and twelve children at No. 10

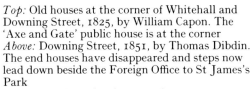

Top: Old houses at the corner of Whitehall and Downing Street, 1825, by William Capon. The 'Axe and Gate' public house is at the corner
Above: Downing Street, 1851, by Thomas Dibdin. The end houses have disappeared and steps now lead down beside the Foreign Office to St James's Park
Above right: Downing Street and government offices, 1857. The present Foreign Office is on the site of the houses on the left

Opposite: Two views of Downing Street in 1827, by J. C. Buckler. Downing Street (*above*) and the Treasury and houses in Downing Street from St James's Park (*below*)

Sir John Soane, who designed the State Dining-room at No. 10, by John Jackson, 1828

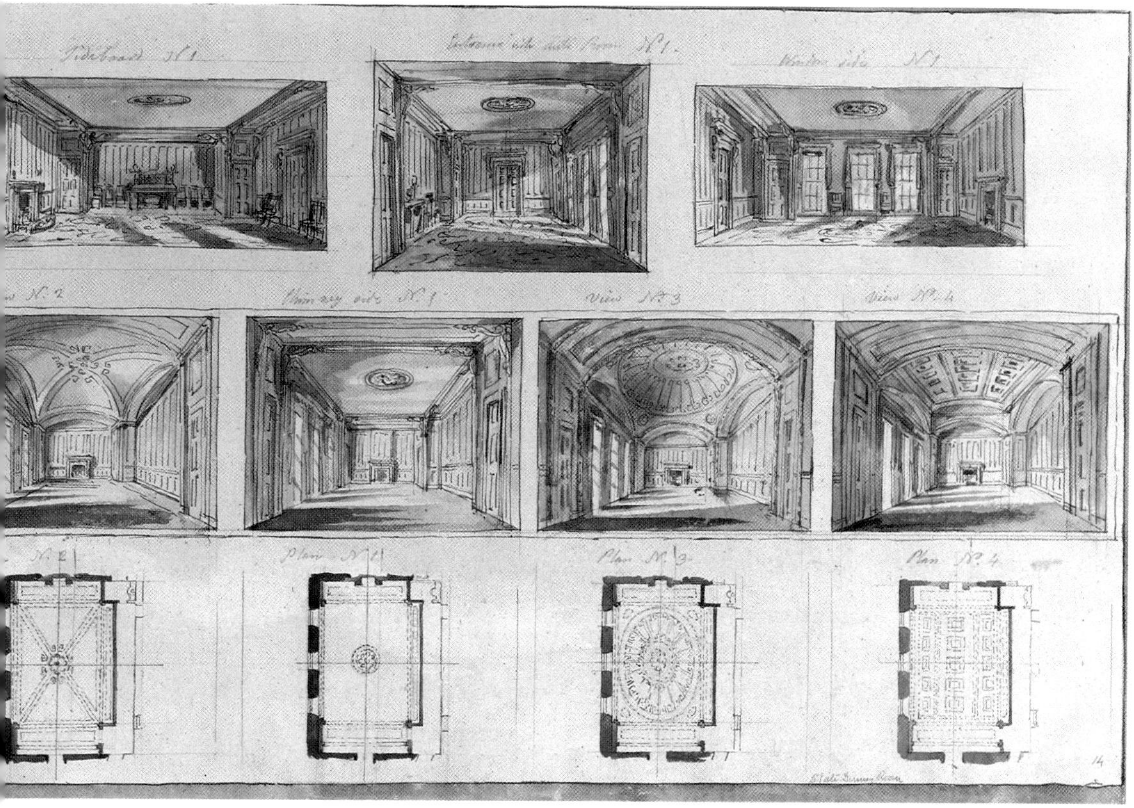

Soane's 1825 designs for the State Dining-room, which he made for the Chancellor of the Exchequer, 'Prosperity' Robinson, who was living there. Robinson chose the first design in the second row

The Duke of Wellington, who lived at No. 10 while his own London home, Apsley House, was being prepared for him. The painting, by James Ward, is in the Blue Drawing-room

'The Field of Battersea', a caricature of the duel between the Duke of Wellington and the Earl of Winchilsea. Neither was injured

George Canning, who lived at No. 10 for only four months, by Thomas Lawrence, completed by Richard Evans, *c.* 1825

Earl Grey, by Benjamin Haydon. The original caption read: '"Shall I resign?" Earl Grey musing after a day's labour in his room, Downing Street. Sketched from life with the furniture, and room of the First Lord of the Treasury faithfully copied'

a ministerial statement of finance'. Thus he earned his nickname of Prosperity Robinson, and No. 10 was called Prosperity House.

With the burden of war at last removed Robinson could think of better ways of spending public money. He obtained a Government grant towards the building of the new British Museum, and a year later, in 1824, the country had a windfall when the Austrians paid back a war loan: half a million went on new churches; £300,000 on Windsor Castle; and £57,000 to buy the Angerstein Collection of thirty-eight pictures which formed the basis of the National Gallery. Robinson was one of the original trustees of the Gallery and was one of those who chose William Wilkins' design for it which still stands in Trafalgar Square.

With so much money available for public grandeur, some of it, naturally enough, had to be spent on 10 Downing Street. In 1825 Robinson called in John Soane, the greatest architect of his day, to make drastic alterations. Soane's work included a fine new dining-room – the present State Dining-room – with a magnificent vaulted ceiling and oak-panelled walls; and a much smaller, less lofty ante-room, used today as a small and more intimate dining-room. All this, together with various other passages and alterations, cost some £2000, and Robinson was anxious to get it finished. On 18 December 1825 he wrote to Soane urging him to have the

> oak panelling in the Dining Room and ante-room varnished *now*, provided it will not prevent me from being able to use the rooms for any considerable length of time. I should wish it to be begun *immediately* & as I understand you that the varnishing itself would take but a few days, I think there is no doubt the rooms will be perfectly useable by the middle of January. I should like to hear from you whether I am wrong on this supposition.

Robinson was wrong, although Soane gave him a worthless assurance that the rooms 'may be varnished fit for his use on or before the middle of January'. They were not, in fact, ready until April. Robinson wrote to Soane in March inviting him to a small party which will 'dine in my new room (for the *first* time) on Tuesday next the 4th April. I wish you would be of the party that you may see how well it looks when lighted up.'

The work on No. 10 went on, in fact, for another three years. In 1829 the Office of Works reported: 'This is a large old Building which has been altered, and added to, at many different periods, and tho' in a substantial condition requires very frequent repairs.'

The nation's economy had become equally rickety and Robinson's prosperity bubble had burst. There was a run on the banks, and many of them failed; wages fell and factories and mills closed their doors to their hungry workers. Robinson, his Midas touch with the economy quite gone, tried to resign, but the increasingly exhausted Lord Liverpool told him to stay on. 'This is the first session you have had of real financial difficulty,' the Prime Minister told him, 'and I do not think it would be for your credit that you should appear to shrink from it.' But in February 1827 Liverpool was found by his servant on the

'Prosperity' Robinson, by Thomas Lawrence, *c.* 1824

floor of his room 'in a violent apoplectic fit, quite senseless', and although he lived for another two years he 'scarcely ever woke to perfect consciousness again'. The King chose George Canning to succeed him, and a number of ministers, including the Duke of Wellington and Peel, who could not stomach Canning's reforming ideas, promptly resigned. Robinson left Downing Street and the new Prime Minister moved in.

Canning was fifty-six, and a very sick man. Lord Eldon had written, after Lord Liverpool's attack, 'I should *suppose* Canning's health would not let him undertake the labour of the situation. But ambition will attempt anything.' And ambition did attempt the ultimate task in British politics. Canning was at No. 10 for just four months before that ambition killed him. He was both Prime Minister and Chancellor of the Exchequer. He had indirectly begun his political career in Downing Street when, as the bright son of a Londonderry-born actress, he had been received at No. 10 by Pitt in August 1792. Pitt was impressed and found him a seat in the Commons. Canning himself remembered the event and being 'ushered into that study in which so many great statesmen and great scoundrels have at different times planned their country's ruin and the advancement of their own futures'. When he finally came to sit in that study himself, Canning had no future. When Liverpool resigned, he said he was too ill in bed with rheumatism even to attend his mother's funeral at Bath, much less take a journey of 100 yards to the Commons. He felt 'ill all over' when he went to No. 10. He could not get rid of the cold that he had earlier caught at the Duke of York's funeral, and in August 1827 he went to stay at the Duke of Devonshire's house at Chiswick. There, in the same room where Charles James Fox had died twenty-one years before, he died on 8 August.

Canning's body was brought back to No. 10; his sufferings had been great. Although his doctors had said, when he went into No. 10, that he had 'stamina for several years to come', only four months later he lay in his coffin there, so 'frightfully attenuated', reported *The Times*, 'that those who are most intimately acquainted with his person would not now recognise it'. His widow Joan, who had nursed him devotedly, invited only 'relatives and medical attendants' to 'attend in Downing St', and to go 'from thence in procession to the Abbey'. Canning's body was laid at the feet of his great friend and mentor, William Pitt.

After this short and unhappy interlude at No. 10, Robinson was brought back, this time as Prime Minister and elevated to the peerage as Viscount Goderich. His jaunty confidence had now quite gone, and he achieved the odd distinction of being Britain's only Prime Minister who never appeared before Parliament. A son, who was to become the Marquess of Ripon, Viceroy of India, was born at No. 10, but Goderich could not cope with office any more. On 8 January 1828 he went to see George IV to offer his resignation. He burst into tears and 'the king offered him his pocket handkerchief'. He stayed on in politics, in other offices, for some years, weeping copiously when the occasion required, and earning himself the unflattering nickname of 'Goody' Goderich.

It is impossible to imagine Goody Goderich's successor weeping, or showing any kind of emotion about anything. The Duke of Wellington did not move immediately into No. 10, but he had transferred himself, his furniture and his devoted but ignored wife to their new home by the middle of August. *The Times* of 5 August 1828: 'Part of the furniture of the Duke of Wellington's residence in Piccadilly was begun to be removed yesterday to the house in Downing-street belonging to His Grace as First Lord of the Treasury, which His Grace, it is expected, will occupy during the time that Apsley House is undergoing repair.' A week later the Duke had left Apsley House 'for his official residence in Downing-street'. Apsley House had been bought by the nation for the Duke from his brother, the Marquess Wellesley, and he remained at No. 10 for eighteen months while it was made into a house fit for the saviour of Europe.

Wellington had, of course, long experience of politics and Downing Street, and he was involved in one of the most remarkable events in the street's history – although not at No. 10. Twenty-three years before he moved into No. 10 as Prime Minister, Wellington had had his only meeting with Nelson in a house which was on the site of what is now the Government Whips' office at No. 12. Although a room in No. 12 is still shown as the room in which they met, the house was rebuilt in the 1960s and is an entirely different building from the one in which the two great leaders came face to face.

That meeting was in September 1805, a few weeks before Nelson was killed at Trafalgar. Wellington had gone to see Lord Castlereagh, the Secretary for War and the Colonies, at the old Colonial Office in Downing Street, and there, in the 'little waiting-room on the right hand', he met a man who, from his pictures and 'the loss of an arm', he took to

Wellington (*left*) and Nelson at their only meeting, in September 1805, after the painting by J. P. Knight

be Nelson. Nelson promptly launched into a monologue, Wellington later recalled, in 'a style so vain and so silly as to surprise and disgust me'. Nelson, however, seemed to be uncertain about the identity of the man he was talking to, and slipped out of the room to check up on him. When he returned his attitude had entirely changed. His 'charlatan manner' had vanished; he talked knowledgeably about events at home and abroad; 'in fact, he talked like an officer and a statesman'. He was 'really a very superior man', but Wellington was still astonished in the change of character that Nelson had shown during their meeting: 'Certainly a more sudden and complete metamorphosis I never saw.'

The Duke's tremendous dignity came within an ace of being very severely disrupted while he was living at No. 10. He had to fight a duel. Catholic emancipation was once again being bitterly argued over in Parliament, and Wellington had come, reluctantly, to support some relief in the rules discriminating against Catholics in public life. A dunderheaded member of the House of Lords, Lord Winchilsea, accused him of an 'insidious design' for the 'introduction of Popery into every department of State'. Winchilsea refused to apologise, and in the early morning of 21 March 1829, Wellington mounted his horse from the mounting-block outside No. 10, and rode off to Battersea Fields to meet his insulter. The Secretary at War, General Sir Henry Hardinge, was his second, and his horrified doctor, Dr Hume, was also there. 'Now then, Hardinge,' barked the Duke, 'look sharp and step out the ground. I have no time to waste. Damn it! Don't stick him up so near the ditch. If I hit him he will tumble in.'

In the event nobody hit anybody. Both men deliberately missed. Lord Falmouth, Winchilsea's very nervous second, produced a piece of paper from his pocket with a ready-written apology on it, and after a good deal of huffing and puffing from the Duke, this was accepted. Wellington got on his horse, raised two fingers to the brim of his hat, snapped 'Good morning, my Lord Winchilsea; good morning, my Lord Falmouth', and rode back to Whitehall.

The duel had taken place nine days before the Catholic Relief Bill had its third reading in the House of Commons. When it went to the Lords, Wellington spoke, his arms folded at the despatch box, for almost an hour in its favour. The Lords followed his lead and the bill was given the Royal Assent on 13 April. 'Well,' said the Duke, the man who had had the wisdom to change his mind, 'I said I would do it, and I have done it handsomely, have I not?'

Like prime ministers before him and since, Wellington accepted the post of Lord Warden of the Cinque Ports, and in the spring of 1829 he went to the Lord Warden's official residence at Walmer Castle. He kept his office in the Cabinet Room at No. 10, but by January 1830 Apsley House was ready for him again, and he lived there for the rest of his time in office.

Wellington lent No. 10 to an old friend, Earl Bathurst, the Lord President of the Council. The death of the king in June 1830 meant a general election, and the Government emerged from it greatly weakened. With the spirit of revolution now abroad in Europe, the demand for parliamentary reform was mounting unstoppably in Britain. Wellington, once the national hero, had to make Apsley House into a fortress and his servants were armed. On 15 November 1830 the Government was defeated on a minor matter, but it was the end of Wellington's administration. The news came when he was at dinner at Apsley House. 'Do not tell the women,' said the Duke. On 16 November he resigned – 'I believe there never was a man suffered so much; and for so little purpose.'

The Whig leader, Lord Grey, formed the new Government, and led the campaign for reform. Earl Grey was sixty-six, a tall and handsome man with fourteen surviving children who, with his wife and grandchildren, brought No. 10 swarming to life again. The old gossip Creevey was at full chat. In January 1831 he 'dined in Downing Street with Lady Grey' and picked the brains of the Prime Minister's private secretary to find out why Lord Grey was not there. He had gone, it transpired, to Brighton to put to William IV his plans for parliamentary reform: 'A ticklish operation this! to propose to a Sovereign a plan for reducing his own power and patronage.' The plan was 'cut and dry' and the Cabinet 'unanimous on the subject'; and Grey found the King all compliance. He 'pledged himself irrevocably' to support his Government, even though Grey's famous charm failed to work on Queen Adelaide. Creevey, however, was quite sure this would not matter; Grey had 'satisfied himself that she has no influence with the King, and that, in fact, he never even mentions politicks to her, much less consults her . . .'

Lady Grey gave pleasant little 'at homes' one evening a week at No. 10, and Creevey, of course, was there. 'I wish you could have been with me when I entered our Premier's drawing-room last night. I was rather early, and he was standing alone with his back to a fire – the best dressed, the handsomest, and apparently the happiest man in all his royal master's dominions . . .'

Sir Robert Peel, by Alfred Crowquill, 1850

Outside that warm and cosy world, however, the political tensions were rising. The mobs were out demanding reform, and once again they swarmed into Downing Street. And once again, as they had been in the Gordon riots more than fifty years before, soldiers were on guard. The mob surged towards the house, bawling their chant of 'Liberty or death'. A soldier cocked his musket at them and roared back: 'Liberty I don't know much about, but if you come any further I'll show you what death is.' The mob quietened down and shuffled off home.

As the dramas of the Reform Bill moved to their climax at Westminster, Grey and his family had to move out of Downing Street to their house at East Sheen. No. 10 was yet again falling down. Workmen once more moved in, and this time the repairs cost a total of £1247. The work took at least three months, and Creevey, of course, bustled round to report on the repairs and decorations to his sister:

I might as well say a word of the new furniture in Downing Street at Earl Grey's, everything therein being all spick and span new. The two principal Drawing Rooms opening into each other are papered with a pattern of your Drawing Room *ground*, and a large *gold* rose or flower of some kind . . . The curtains are yellow silk . . . as gay and handsome as possible.

But Grey was becoming more and more exhausted with his struggles to get reform through Parliament, and his Government became prey to 'blunders and embarrassments'. Servants spread gossip they had picked up at Cabinet dinners, and the Cabinet itself began to disintegrate. In the summer of 1834 Grey resigned. 'My life for the past eight months has been one of such unhappiness as nobody can imagine . . .' He left Downing Street when he was seventy years old, the last Prime Minister to live there for over thirty years.

Eight prime ministers totally ignored No. 10. Fourteen administrations came and went before the house became, once again, the centre of government. At first senior civil servants were given the house by their political masters – with fatal consequences to one of them – and the state rooms were used for formal entertaining; but for thirty years, from 1847 to 1877, no one lived there at all; it was just a block of offices.

Sir Robert Peel, during both his administrations, stayed on at his equally convenient house at Whitehall Gardens, and in 1842 he lent

'Lady John Russell's Assembly on Wednesday evening, at Downing Street – The Refreshment Room', 1850

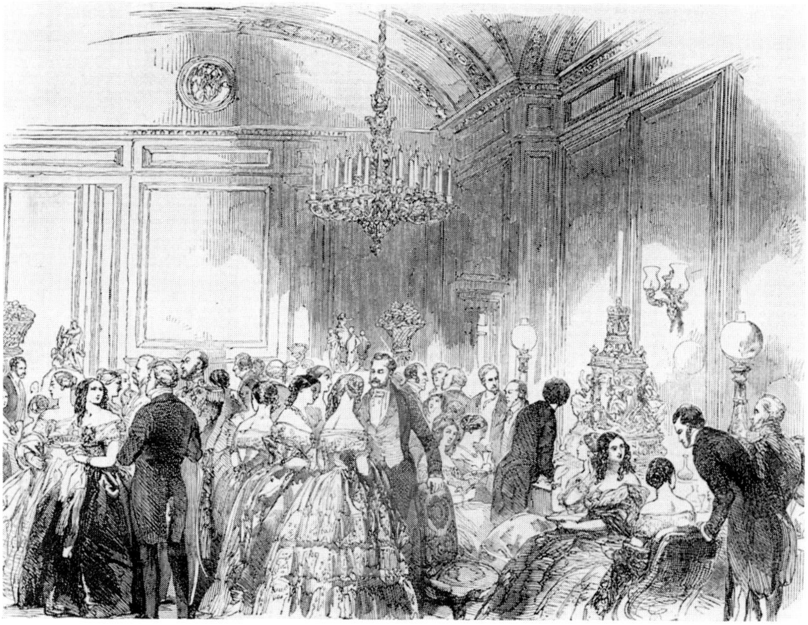

the house to Edward Drummond, his private secretary, who had also been secretary to Canning and Wellington before him. This act of kindness by Peel cost Drummond his life. The house was being watched by a deranged 27-year-old Irishman, Daniel Macnaghten, who had a persecution mania about the Pope, the Jesuits and Sir Robert Peel. Macnaghten, 'well, though not genteely dressed', said *The Times*, had spent a couple of weeks hovering outside No. 10, and decided that Drummond was Sir Robert Peel. On 20 January 1843, Drummond went to visit his brother at his bank at Charing Cross. Macnaghten followed him, and as Drummond passed the Admiralty on his way back to Downing Street, he walked up behind him and shot him in the back; Drummond died five days later. As he was hauled off to prison, Macnaghten mumbled: 'He shall not disturb my mind any longer.' His trial was to make British legal history: he was found 'not guilty by reason of insanity', and rules were laid down – the 'Macnaghten Rules' – governing the criminal responsibility of the insane. Queen Victoria was much upset; she had, after all, been shot at three times by madmen. 'Poor Drummond is universally regretted,' she wrote to her uncle, King Leopold of the Belgians. 'People can hardly think of anything else.'

Daniel Macnaghten

People, in fact, were probably not much surprised, since the whole area round Downing Street – and Downing Street itself – had been going steadily downhill for years. By the early 1800s the street had become 'a dingy solitary street with a dirty public house on the corner and a row of third-rate lodging houses between it and the Foreign Office', and the Foreign Office, which was across the road from No. 10, was itself dilapidated and run-down. Three years after Drummond's assassination there were 170 brothels and 145 gin parlours in the parishes of St Margaret and St John, and slum-clearance schemes simply forced the poor to crowd even closer together in the wretched hovels that remained. The dreadful indignity of trade even invaded Downing Street itself. When Palmerston was Foreign Secretary, he received a complaint from a milliner who had her establishment in the street that clerks in the Foreign Office were amusing themselves by flashing mirrors into her young ladies' eyes as they sat sewing by her windows. Palmerston scribbled in the margin of the letter of complaint: 'Who are the unmannerly youths who have been casting reflections on young ladies opposite?' The reflections stopped.

In spite of its rather seedy appearance, Downing Street had become more and more the centre of all government activity. The Colonial Office had moved into No. 14 in 1798; the Foreign Office was at No. 16, and gradually absorbed houses on either side; the West India Department was in No. 18; and the Tithe Commissioners were in No. 20. The Government spent over £61,000 buying up the freeholds, and knocked much of the rickety property down. Most of it, except No. 10 and Nos. 11 and 12, had gone by 1857. The Chancellor's house at No. 11 had had a good deal spent on it to make it more habitable; nearly £4000 was spent in 1847 to make it 'more convenient both for Official purposes and for the residence of a Family, by allotting separate portions for each object, instead of continuing the mixed occupation which has existed'.

In No. 10 there were no families – just the clerks who now scurried round its corridors and up and down its staircase. Disraeli ignored the place when he became Prime Minister in February 1868; Gladstone, when he formed his administration in December of the same year, remained in his house in Carlton House Terrace. In 1874 Disraeli defeated his great Liberal antagonist and was in office again. For two years he remained at his house in Whitehall Gardens, but then, in November 1877, he moved to No. 10 and the old house was once again the official home of the British Prime Minister.

CHAPTER EIGHT

'My Lone, Rambling House'

Downing Street did not impress the Victorians. Most of the Queen-Empress's prime ministers were wealthy aristocrats who much preferred to remain in their own splendid residences rather than squash in with the clerks in a Westminster back street. Some prime ministers had their office there, and kept a spare bed in case there were late-night sittings at the Commons; even those who moved into the house did so simply because it was cheaper or more convenient. The street had still not achieved its aura of possessing an immutable place in history or of being the very highest pinnacle of political success. That did not come until the early years of the twentieth century. Even the Cabinet met at No. 10 only when the Prime Minister wished it to do so. Frequently it met in the Foreign Office immediately across the street, and when the FO was grandly rebuilt in the 1870s, it included a magnificent Cabinet Room, much bigger and more splendid than the one in No. 10.

After Grey left office in 1834, Melbourne, Peel, Russell, Derby, Aberdeen and Palmerston all avoided No. 10, and Disraeli and Gladstone ignored the place until their second terms of office. It was not until Balfour became Prime Minister in 1902 – he had already been living there for seven years as First Lord of the Treasury – that the firm tradition of all Prime Ministers taking up residence was at last established. Downing Street itself had been made a little more civilised when in 1831 the road surface was macadamised, using the system invented by the young Scottish engineer, John Macadam, twenty years before. The cost to the taxpayer was £190 11s. 6d.

Benjamin Disraeli had already spent one brief period in office when he became Prime Minister for the second time in 1874. The Queen was delighted, and letters of deep affection went almost daily to and fro between the sovereign and her Prime Minister. That delight knew no bounds when in 1875, with brilliant daring, Disraeli pulled off the great financial coup of buying the shares in the Suez Canal from the bankrupt Kedive of Egypt. The money was lent to the Government, without parliamentary approval, by the Rothschilds – 'Tis an affair of millions; about four at least', wrote Disraeli to the Queen – and although Disraeli was not then living at No. 10, discussions went on there for days about whether or not to risk the venture. Disraeli's secretary waited outside the Cabinet Room for instructions. Finally, the door opened; Disraeli put his head out and said 'Yes', and without further explanation the secretary went off to settle the arrangements with the Rothschild bank. It was, wrote the Queen, 'an immense thing', since it gave Britain absolute security of the route to India.

Benjamin Disraeli

In November 1877 Disraeli decided to move into No. 10 from his house in Whitehall Gardens. His wife had died five years before, and with her had gone a good deal of his income. He was becoming more and more wretched in his loneliness, and ill-health was beginning to make his life intolerable. The year before he moved, the Queen had created him Earl of Beaconsfield, at least partly in the hope that the House of Lords would be less demanding of his time and energy than the Commons.

The bowls of primroses which the Queen sent to Disraeli at No. 10 – she knew they were his favourite flowers – were not enough to brighten up the cheerless rooms which had been empty for decades. Disraeli demanded expensive renovations. The Treasury was horrified. The cost of decorating one of the state rooms came to £782, and warning letters began to fly. The Lords of the Treasury would 'regret to see any greater outlay incurred than is absolutely essential for placing the room in a condition appropriate to the uses for which it was designed'. And it would be 'injudicious to spend any large amount upon so old a house and one in which the approaches and other arrangements are so decidedly defective'. But the vexed matter of who should pay for the furniture at No. 10 was also finally settled. A Treasury minute of May 1878, six months after Disraeli had moved in, said that as the entrance-hall, staircase and first-floor rooms were for public use they would be

A Cabinet Council, January 1877. Disraeli is third from the right

furnished at public expense. In the rest of the house, however, the Prime Minister would have to pay for the wear and tear and repair of the furniture that was officially provided for him – and in Disraeli's case this was a good deal. The furniture in the main reception room cost well over £1000, including silk-covered chairs and sofas, silk curtains, a number of tables and fine rugs and carpets. But still Disraeli was not satisfied that the neglect of the house had been sufficiently dispelled. There was more work done on the drawing-room, and on the 'First Lord's Official room, Bedroom, Dressing-room and ante-room, with Plate-glass for windows in Official rooms £400'. There was also 'Bath with hot and cold water in First Lord's Dressing room £150', and what with the 'necessary painting, cleansing, whitewashing', it all came to a further £2350. All this for what Disraeli called his 'lone, rambling house'.

Disraeli was almost always unwell there. He was wracked by gout, rheumatism and asthma, and sometimes the asthma was so bad that he had to spend all night sitting in one chair while leaning on the back of another. As he wrote of his afflictions: 'When one has got everything in the world one ever wished for, and is prostrate with pain or debility, one knows the value of health...'

He was also the victim of one of those crosses that all occupants of No. 10 have to bear – the over-persistent admirer. This was a man with the decidedly odd name of Tracy Turnerelli, who arrived constantly on the doorstep asking to meet his hero. He had collected what he called 'The People's Tribute' to the great man – 52,000 pennies which he had used to buy a gold wreath, which he wanted to place on the Prime Minister's brow above his famous quiff. Turnerelli was, time and again, patiently turned away, but then one day, when he was walking along Bond Street, he suddenly came face to face with Disraeli. He rushed up to him, and announced he was 'the unfortunate Tracy Turnerelli'. Disraeli shook him by the hand and said amiably, 'You have now got what you desired.' Turnerelli had, of course, got no such thing. He had imagined himself presenting the gold wreath, which was exhibited at the Crystal Palace, in a blaze of publicity at No. 10; all he had got was a quick handshake in the street. As for the wreath, it never reached No. 10 but wound up in Madame Tussaud's waxworks.

Disraeli, though, had a triumph at No. 10 far greater than the dotty Mr Turnerelli could ever have imagined. Russia was threatening the peace and stability of Europe with ever-increasing imperial ambitions. The Queen was warning Disraeli about the need for '*preventing* the Russians' from reaching Constantinople. War seemed more and more likely, as orders were given for 7000 Indian troops to be ready to embark for Turkey. Two of Disraeli's Cabinet, including Lord Derby, the Foreign Secretary, resigned, and preparations for war grew. In January 1878 the British fleet was ordered to Constantinople and an extra £6 million was voted for armaments. In the face of this determination – be 'very firm', said the Queen – Russia was ready to come to the conference table in Berlin. Disraeli left Downing Street for the

Conference of Berlin on 8 June 1878, assuring the Queen that 'In all his troubles and perplexities, he will think of his Sovereign Lady, and that thought will sustain and inspire him'. The Queen did not want him to go; she was worried about the effect the strain of the conference and the long journeys would have on his health. Disraeli, however, not only went, but scored a considerable triumph. He had threatened to walk out at one stage when the Russians were being obstinate, but his ploy worked, and he was able to cable the Queen: 'Russia surrenders and accepts the English scheme for the European frontier of the Empire ...' The Queen was overwhelmed: 'It's all due to your energy and firmness,' she wrote, and Disraeli gave her the present of Cyprus to add to her empire.

Mr and Mrs Gladstone, *c.* 1890. They knelt to pray together in the entrance-hall of No. 10 after they heard the news of the Phoenix Park murders in 1882

Disraeli returned to London on 16 July in triumph. Charing Cross station was smothered in crimson hangings and great banks of flowers, and Downing Street itself had been hung with scarlet. Vast crowds cheered him all the way into the house, and the Queen's secretary waited for him there with a bouquet of flowers. The Foreign Secretary, Lord Salisbury, was with him. The roar of the crowd drew the Prime Minister to a window. He leant out and called to them: 'Lord Salisbury and myself have brought you back peace, but a peace, I hope, with honour.' Like that other declaration from a window at No. 10 sixty years later that reflected those words, it proved to be a hollow promise. For Russia, cheated in Europe, turned its attention to Afghanistan and drew Britain into two years of bloody fighting.

Less than two years after his great triumph in Berlin, Disraeli was voted out of office by the British electorate. There had been war not only in Afghanistan, but against the Zulus in South Africa; at home there were bad harvests, bankruptcies, unemployment, and hunger in Ireland. Gladstone launched his brilliant Midlothian campaign to get the Conservatives out of office. With consuming energy he went on his 'pilgrimage of passion', denouncing Disraeli's imperialism and demanding 'freedom, justice, humanity'. By-election results for the government, however, were quite good, and in March 1880 Disraeli went to the country. The result, for him, was a disaster. The Conservatives lost 111 seats, and Gladstone followed him into No. 10. A year later, on 19 April 1881, Disraeli was dead, with primroses the Queen had sent him in a vase by his bed.

The widowed queen dreaded the return of the dour, square-jawed William Ewart Gladstone. She would, she said, 'sooner *abdicate*' than send for 'that *half-mad fire-brand* who would soon ruin everything, and be a Dictator'. Her son Prince Arthur, however, calmed her down – he wrote that he knew 'how nobly you can sacrifice your own feelings at the call of duty' – and Mr Gladstone turned out to be not quite such an ogre after all. The Queen got herself firmly under control when he went to kiss hands. She received him with 'perfect courtesy', and was, said Gladstone, 'natural under effort'.

Gladstone, Prime Minister for the second time, at the age of seventy-one moved not only into No. 10 but into Nos. 11 and 12 as well. He used No. 10 as his office – his grand piano was installed there for his daughter to play to him – but his son, Herbert Gladstone MP, moved into the main part of the house, and Gladstone and his wife and servants seem to have spread themselves round the other two houses. There was the inevitable official fussing about the cost of the furniture: five days after Disraeli moved out, the First Commissioner of Works reported that the cost of the furniture supplied to Mr Gladstone was £1555 5s. 'As it was absolutely necessary that all the things should be provided at once, it was not possible to report the sum before the expenditure was incurred,' he added in a determined attempt to cover his own tracks.

Gladstone had some sort of claim to occupying so much of Downing Street since he was Chancellor of the Exchequer as well as Prime Minister. 'I have not sufficient confidence in the financial judgment of my colleagues,' he explained. The work load he imposed on himself was formidable. Although he withdrew British troops from Afghanistan, war threatened once more in the Balkans and he ordered a naval demonstration off the coast of Albania. He waited tensely to see if this threat had had the necessary effect on the Turks, who were trying to undermine the provisions of the Treaty of Berlin. It did, and the Foreign Secretary, Lord Granville, hurried to No. 10 with the happy news. He hopped around the Prime Minister's desk – the same one that Disraeli used – and 'danced very gracefully upon his toes, waving his arms and brandishing his copy of the telegram. At last Gladstone looked up, and the Foreign Secretary for a full minute continued to dance and to enjoy the Prime Minister's gaze of utter stupefaction. Then he handed him the message. "God Almighty be praised!" Gladstone exclaimed. "I can catch the 2.45 to Hawarden."'

But the problems of office soon enough dragged Gladstone back from his country home at Hawarden and his relaxation of chopping down trees on his estate. Family tragedy struck at No. 10 through the insoluble problems of Ireland. In his desperate attempts to bring peace and prosperity to that country, Gladstone brought in the Land Bill which he had designed to help the Irish tenants. Like so many other attempts to do good in Ireland, this one stirred up anger and conflict there, resulting in the arrest of Charles Stewart Parnell, the leader of the Irish National Party in the Commons. On 6 May 1882 Parnell was freed, and it was hoped he would help to restore law and order in his country. Four days later these hopes were utterly dashed with the murder in Phoenix Park, Dublin, of the new Irish Secretary, Lord Frederick Cavendish, and Thomas Burke, the Permanent Under Secretary. They were both stabbed to death.

Lord Frederick Cavendish was a nephew of Mrs Gladstone's by marriage and a particular favourite of Gladstone himself, who 'loved him like a son'. The Prime Minister and his wife had been out to dinner at the Austrian Embassy on the evening of the murder. He walked back to Downing Street afterwards, while Mrs Gladstone went to a party at the Admiralty. When she arrived at the Admiralty she was immediately asked to hurry back to No. 10. There she was met by her husband's secretary who told her the terrible news. When Gladstone arrived back he heard their conversation. He felt as though he had been 'felled to the ground', and clasping his wife's hand he knelt, with her beside him, on the black and white marble floor of the entrance-hall to pray. Then they called their carriage and drove from Downing Street to comfort Lord Frederick's wife at her home in Carlton House Terrace. Gladstone was, she said, 'like an oak to lean against'.

He was, presumably, a good deal less sympathetic when, a few months later, Mrs Kitty O'Shea twice visited him at No. 10. The scandal of Parnell's adultery with Mrs O'Shea was, some years later, to be his ruin; but only a few months after the Phoenix Park murders she tried to bring about some sort of understanding between the Prime Minister and her lover. Gladstone received her in his room at No. 10 and, according to her own account, walked up and down the room with her, arm in arm. Perhaps Mrs O'Shea's version of their meetings was a little coloured, but Gladstone certainly came to admire Parnell and thought he was 'fit for the leadership of a nation'. After the scandal of his divorce, however, Gladstone thought it would be a disaster for Ireland if Parnell were to continue in politics.

Gladstone's own career was nearly wrecked, certainly not by anything remotely suggesting moral lapses, but by lapses of political judgment which led to the death of the national hero, General Gordon, at Khartoum. Gladstone had been unwilling to become involved in an uprising in the Sudan which he saw as a move, led by the Mahdi and his dervishes, against their Egyptian oppressors. Britain, as the great power in the area, was, however, inexorably drawn in, and General Gordon was sent to Khartoum to establish stable government there. The Mahdi's defeated forces regrouped and, while Gladstone dithered, descended on Khartoum; on 26 January 1885 they slaughtered Gordon on the steps of the Palace. The Queen blazed with anger; it had been her Prime Minister's duty, she said, to save him. When he arrived back at Downing Street on the day the terrible news arrived, Gladstone found a telegram waiting him from her. 'These news from Khartoum are frightful,' she said, rather oddly, 'and to think that all this might have been prevented and many precious lives saved by earlier action is too frightful.' The nation agreed with her. Gladstone was roundly booed by the crowds as he went from Downing Street to the Commons.

He thought the death of Gordon might bring down his Government, but it was able to struggle on until June. He was defeated by an alliance of the Irish members with the Conservatives against the budget on 8 June 1885. He sent his resignation to the Queen next day. 'What a relief!' she confided to her journal, and sent for Lord Salisbury to form a Government.

This great lord had no intention of moving into No. 10. He created the Conservative leader in the Commons, Sir Stafford Northcote, the new First Lord of the Treasury – with, of course, the house and the salary which went with the job. As the new tenant entered the house,

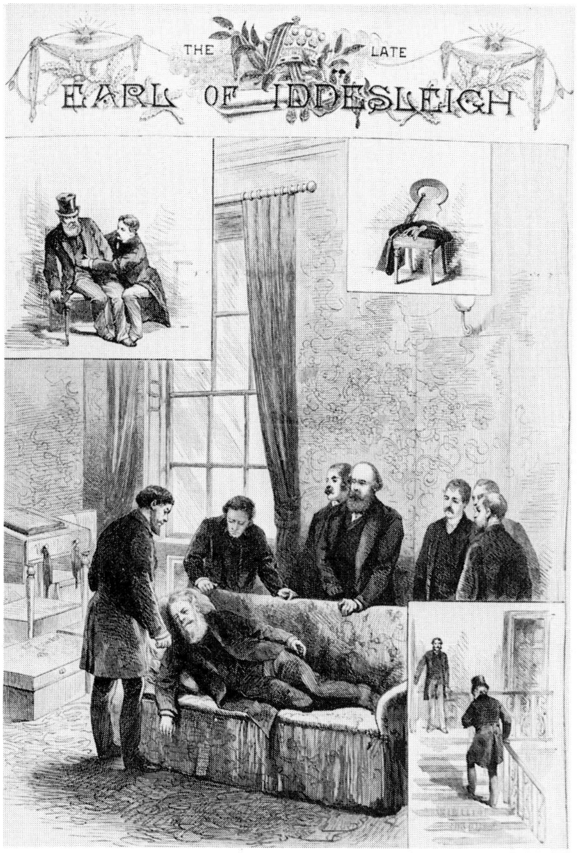

Above: Downing Street, *c.* 1880, photographed by Francis Frith. This photograph is now in the entrance-hall of No. 10

Left: The death of Lord Iddesleigh, 11 January 1887

the old tenant was moving out. Gladstone was coming down the great staircase as Northcote – who had once been his private secretary at the Board of Trade – went up. Gladstone was 'very civil' to him and gave him three books of Homer. Northcote, however, hardly had time to find a place on the bookshelves for his new volumes. Salisbury was out of office in seven months and Northcote had to take his old bones – he was sixty-seven – elsewhere. Gladstone moved back in – but only for six months. In August 1886 Salisbury was Prime Minister again.

Northcote had been given the title of Lord Iddesleigh when he became First Lord, and soon the eldest of his ten children was to inherit it. Iddesleigh paid a visit to No. 10 on 11 January 1887. He got to the top of the staircase on which he had once met Mr Gladstone and collapsed. He was carried into the room the Prime Minister was using as an office – it is now the White Drawing-room – and there he died. The Queen was 'dreadfully grieved'.

The tenant of the house at the time of Iddesleigh's death was Mr W.H. Smith, whom Lord Salisbury, during his second administration, had appointed the First Lord of the Treasury. William Henry Smith was born over his father's newsagent shop in the Strand in 1825; his father had made his fortune by setting up bookstalls on railway

W. H. Smith, the 'son' of W. H. Smith and Son

stations, and took his young son into the business – the 'son' of W.H. Smith and Son. The family and their business prospered, and the son entered politics in 1868. He became Financial Secretary to the Treasury in 1874, and First Lord of the Admiralty in 1877, a fact which W.S. Gilbert gleefully lampooned in *HMS Pinafore*. Smith became Sir Joseph Porter, KCB, who stuck close to his desk and never went to sea, so he became the ruler of the Queen's Navee! In fact Smith, the first man 'in trade' ever to be the tenant of No. 10, was immensely popular with his fellow politicians, and a much-respected Leader of the House of Commons. He was given the nickname of Old Morality, and earned the trust and respect of the Queen: '... I must say I thought him most pleasant, kind and sympathetic, a man to whom one could speak very openly.' He eventually became Lord Warden of the Cinque Ports – 'No one deserves it more than he does,' said the Queen – and died at his official residence at Walmer Castle, exhausted from overwork, in October 1891.

A.J. Balfour moved into No. 10 for the first time as Smith's successor. This time he was there for only a year; when he returned he would be the tenant for ten years. He was Salisbury's nephew, and his uncle now made him Leader of the Commons and First Lord of the Treasury. At forty-three he was a rather languid bachelor of self-conscious artistic

Robert Gascoyne-Cecil, third Marquess of Salisbury

tastes, and very much one of the smart set. The Queen enjoyed the daily reports of Parliament that it was his job to write for her, and the Commons quickly realised that he was a man of formidable ability. But by the time those abilities were being put to good use his uncle was out of office and the Queen had once again, and to her undisguised fury, to send for Mr Gladstone.

As Gladstone's furniture and his piano were once again trundled back into No. 10, the workmen were back there too. Nearly £1780 was spent on renovations and furniture, and generally trying to make the place comfortable for an old man of eighty-three. He was half-blind and very deaf, and the Queen – who was herself seventy-four – saw a 'weird look in his eyes, a feeble expression about the mouth'. He was, she thought, 'no longer fitted to be head of a government'.

The Queen was wrong. Gladstone was determined to make one more attempt to settle the Irish question and to get a home rule bill through Parliament. He worked on it tirelessly, both at Hawarden and at No. 10, for hours on end, scribbling away at his desk lit by its lamp with a green glass shade. He launched the bill in the Commons on 13 February 1893, watched by an awe-struck 18-year-old Winston Churchill. 'The Grand Old Man looked like a great white eagle, at once fierce and splendid', he wrote later. 'His sentences rolled forth majestically and everyone hung upon his lips and gestures, eager to cheer or to deride.' The Commons passed the bill comfortably; the Lords threw it out by 419 to 41. Gladstone wanted to go to the country, but was persuaded not to.

Members of his own Cabinet could not pluck up courage to ask the old man to give up office, but on 1 March 1894 Gladstone presided over his last Cabinet at No. 10. When he announced his decision to resign some of his colleagues broke down, but Gladstone himself was 'composed and still as marble'. He spoke briefly and then said, in a faint whisper, 'God bless you all', and walked out of the room. The rest of the Cabinet filed out through another door. He died four years later, remembering those colleagues who had wept at his going as 'that blubbering Cabinet'.

Archibald Philip Primrose, fifth Earl of Rosebery

The Queen persuaded a reluctant Lord Rosebery to follow Gladstone, but although he had a bedroom at No. 10 he preferred to stay at his splendid town house in Berkeley Square, until repairs there forced him to move to his official residence. He had been present at what he called the 'horrid scene' of Gladstone's farewell (he had been Foreign Secretary), and he was to hold the Premiership himself for sixteen months before Salisbury was once again back in office. 'I am very homesick for the Foreign Office,' he said, 'and I do not think I shall like any of the duties of my new position – patronage is odious.'

Rosebery had the distinction of twice winning the Derby while he was at No. 10 – with Ladas in 1894 and Sir Visto in 1895 (he also won in 1905). The wins were among the few pleasures he had during his term in office. Like many other Prime Ministers before and since, he slept very badly and he went to Epsom to recuperate. While he was there, his Government was defeated on a debate on the Army Esti-

A. J. Balfour at No. 10 in 1905. He was the first Prime Minister to have a car

mates; he had already been commanded to have dinner with the Queen at Windsor that night, and when he arrived he handed her his resignation. He was, he told her, relieved to give up his office and 'the unfortunate inheritance of Mr Gladstone'.

Balfour now returned for his long tenancy of No. 10, again as First Lord of the Treasury and Leader of the Commons under his uncle, Lord Salisbury; and then, in 1902, succeeding him as Prime Minister. He established finally, 167 years after Robert Walpole first moved in, the firm principle that Prime Ministers invariably live at 10 Downing Street.

Salisbury used to hold his Cabinet meetings in the Foreign Office. During the rebuilding in the latter part of the nineteenth century, a magnificent Cabinet room, 70 feet long by 35 feet wide, had been built to replace the one that had already existed in the old, demolished building. It had a round table with twenty leather-upholstered chairs (the Prime Minister's chair was the only one with arms); the ceiling was high and elaborately painted and moulded; and above the great marble fireplace hung a life-size portrait of Queen Victoria.

Balfour used to stroll across from No. 10 to attend the Cabinet meetings there, and during the crisis of the Boer War he would go across to see the latest telegrams the Foreign Office had received. They all too often had bad news, and when he told the Queen (who was by now eighty) about them when he visited her at Windsor, he was given a very thorough dressing-down. 'Please understand that there is no one depressed in this house,' she intoned. 'We are not interested in the possibilities of defeat. They do not exist.'

For Balfour, however, the war seemed a very long way away. He

Above: Balfour's stand-up desk which he used in the Cabinet Room

wrote, unfeelingly, about the 'unhappy entanglement of Ladysmith', and said that there had been 'no great reverses in this war'. *The Times* called him 'irritating'. He had, however, a diverting new toy: he brought the first motor-car to No. 10. He became the owner of a De Dion Voiturette, but some of his enthusiasm was dampened when he and some friends came up from the country by car in the summer of 1900. They had, he said, a 'mild breakdown every three miles', so instead of put-putting to the door of No. 10 in grand style, they finished their journey in a hansom cab.

Balfour resigned in December 1905 and the last Liberal reign at No. 10 began; but it began in an atmosphere of deep sadness and distress. After the elegant sophistication of the Balfour years, his successor, Sir Henry Campbell-Bannerman, was a man heaped with personal sorrows. Asquith was later to call him 'the least cynical of mankind, but no one had a keener eye for the humours and ironies of the political situation'. His tragedy was that his beloved wife was dying as they moved into No. 10. She had been ill and often in great pain for years; for weeks on end he would sleep in a chair by her bed at night instead of going to bed himself. When they moved in she called No. 10 a 'house of doom', and for her husband it was precisely that.

Lady Campbell-Bannerman, however, knew her duty, and she insisted on giving a large party in the state rooms, receiving her guests in great pain, propped in a chair. In August 1906 she went, as she

Below: The Cabinet Room in 1904. Balfour used it as his private office. His desk is by the far window

Balfour moves out of No. 10 in December 1905

usually did, to Marienbad for the waters, and there she died. Her body was brought back, first to No. 10, and then taken for burial to Scotland.

Campbell-Bannerman was inconsolable. The childless couple had been married for forty-five years, and less than a month after his wife's death he had a heart attack. In spite of an overall majority of 132 in the Commons, the Liberal Government was facing growing difficulty with the Lords, which objected to its plans for education. 'The British people must be master in their own house,' declared Sir Henry, as he prepared for a long constitutional fight with their Lordships. He had more heart attacks – his secretary sat in the Commons with a despatch box full of first-aid kit in case it should be needed – and early in 1908 he caught 'flu. On 12 February he had another heart attack at No. 10. Edward VII called to see him, arriving privately at the garden door, then up the terrace steps and in through the French windows of the Cabinet Room. Campbell-Bannerman was helped to his armchair, and he and the King talked together while his nurse sat outside the door. Queen Alexandra drove to the front door to inquire after his health and brought bunches of violets for him. On 4 April 1908 Campbell-Bannerman resigned, and on 22 April he died in his bedroom at No. 10 – the room that is now used by the Prime Minister as her study.

Sir Henry Campbell-Bannerman

Herbert Asquith, the Chancellor of the Exchequer, had effectively been acting as Prime Minister for some time before Campbell-Bannerman's death, and now he took over the office officially, and he, with his formidable wife Margot and their brood of children, moved from No. 11 into No. 10. A few hours before Campbell-Bannerman had died, Asquith had gone through the connecting doors between the two houses to see him. 'Asquith, you are different from the others and I am glad to have known you . . . God bless you' were the parting words between the two Prime Ministers. In fact, Asquith had by then already seen the King and had a 'satisfactory interview' with him.

Above: Margot Asquith with her son Anthony

Right: The wedding of Violet Asquith and Maurice Bonham Carter, Asquith's Private Secretary, in 1915. The wedding group, which was taken in the Cabinet Room, also includes Asquith

Asquith was fifty-six and twice married. After the death of his first wife Helen (their four children included the future Lady Violet Bonham Carter, Baroness Asquith), he married Margot Tennant, one of the twelve children of Sir Charles Tennant, a wealthy Scottish industrialist. Sir Charles had married again in his seventies, and produced four more children who added to the happy family atmosphere that now, once again, swept through No. 10. One of Sir Charles' second family, now Baroness Elliot of Harwood, remembers the atmosphere well. She was taken to No. 10 as a small girl of seven or eight to be with her young relatives – Asquith's second family, a daughter Elizabeth and a son, Anthony, who was later to become the famous film director, and who then was always known as 'Puffin' or 'Puff'. 'No. 10 in those days was a family house,' Baroness Elliot recalls. 'There was only one floor where we didn't run about. That was the entertaining floor with the lovely drawing-room and dining-room. We used to run about all over the place, but we didn't go in there unless we were asked.'

Sometimes they *were* asked. Margot Asquith used to give grand lunches and dinner parties in the state rooms, when she dressed herself in the height of fashion. There was a crowd of servants, and the whole thing was organised by an imperturbable butler. The small children were, on occasions, brought in to meet the terrifying guests. Margot, who was marvellous with children, arranged for them to have their meal, with their governess and nanny, first in the small dining-room. 'There would be an enormous lunch party going on next door,' recalls Lady Elliot, 'and then before we left, Margot used to come in and would make us all go round and shake hands with all these grand people, which was extremely alarming.'

When the children could get away from such splendid grown-ups, they enjoyed themselves thoroughly in No. 10's garden. In 1909 Louis Blériot flew the Channel, and model aeroplanes became the latest toy. Puff and the young Katherine used to fly these paper and wood creations, powered by elastic bands, in the garden; when they went over the wall into Horse Guards, the long-suffering policemen brought them back; when they crashed into the trees and bushes, Margot rescued them and complained about tearing her dresses on the sooty branches. Sometimes she had to dodge when the ebullient Puff whizzed round the garden paths on his roller-skates.

No. 10 in 1904
Above: The White Drawing-room, which was Balfour's study and music room
Below: The Blue Drawing-room

Above: The State Dining-room, with two of Edward Burne-Jones's paintings
Below: The Pillared Drawing-room. A portrait of Walpole hangs over the fireplace

Suffragettes had already made No. 10 a target for their rowdy demonstrations in Campbell-Bannerman's day, with the Pankhursts and Mrs 'General' Drummond leading the crowds, and their followers chaining themselves to the railings outside the famous front door. They continued with their uproar when Asquith took over.

I was quite young [recalls Lady Elliot], and I can remember going to No. 10 to stay there with Puff and being taken through the front door – which was being picketed by Suffragettes – by my nanny, and then led into No. 10. I may say, had I been older I would have been a Suffragette, but on that occasion I was only seven years old, and I didn't really know what was happening. And then we did a really naughty thing: when we got to the nursery, which was on the third floor, Puff and I took a large teddy bear and threw it out of the window on to the Suffragettes below.

The young Violet Asquith was enjoying herself, too. She never got back to No. 10 from dances, she recalled, until the small hours. 'I remember going to the window very drowsily in the morning and seeing the young men I had danced with hanging up their bowler hats and umbrellas across the road at the Foreign Office.'

Margot Asquith called the outside of No. 10 'liver-coloured and squalid', and said it gave little idea to the man in the street of what it was really like. What was increasingly going on within those drab walls, in the solemnity of the Cabinet Room behind the double doors which made it sound-proof from prying ears, was the grim preparation for war. In July 1914 Margot sent a telegram to her daughter in Holland telling her to come home. The Archbishop of Canterbury, a dinner guest at No. 10, was surprised at her action. Wasn't she overdoing things? As the crisis grew, Asquith drove from No. 10 to Buckingham Palace at one o'clock in the morning to keep King George V informed of developments. On the night of 4 August Asquith (who was also Secretary of State for War), Churchill (the First Lord of the Admiralty), Sir Edward Grey (the Foreign Secretary), and Margot Asquith were with other ministers in the Cabinet Room, waiting for the clock on the white marble mantelpiece to strike midnight.

Suffragettes chained themselves to the railings of No. 10 in January 1908

CHAPTER NINE

War to War

For the group of people who gathered in the Cabinet Room late in the evening of 4 August 1914 it was the culmination of a tense and dramatic day. The Prime Minister and his wife had only just returned to Downing Street from the House of Commons. There Margot Asquith had gone up to the Ladies Gallery, and 'glued her face to the grille' to look down over the heads of the journalists in the Press Gallery to her husband speaking at the Despatch Box. He told the crowded House that Germany had been sent an ultimatum that morning to respect the neutrality of Belgium, and that the ultimatum expired at midnight. Through Margot's 'misty eyes' the 'heads of the listening members appeared to me as if bowed in prayer'.

The Asquiths went back to No. 10 through crowds of sightseers. There Margot thought first of her duties as a mother.

> I looked at the children asleep after dinner before joining Henry in the Cabinet Room. Lord Crewe and Sir Edward Grey were already there and we sat smoking cigarettes in silence; some went out; others came in; nothing was said. The clock on the mantelpiece hammered out the hour and when the last beat of midnight struck it was as silent as dawn. We were at war. I left to go to bed, and, as I was pausing at the foot of the staircase, I saw Winston Churchill with a happy face striding towards the double doors of the Cabinet Room.

David Lloyd George was already living in No. 11. He and his family had moved in there when he was appointed Chancellor of the Exchequer in 1908. He drastically increased taxes – he doubled income tax to 2s. 8d. in the pound (13.3 per cent) – to pay for the war effort. In 1915 Asquith set up a Coalition Government and Lloyd George became Minister of Munitions, a new post created to deal with shortage of supplies for the troops, but he stayed on in No. 11. Lord Kitchener remained Secretary of State for War, but when he was killed in June 1916 when HMS *Hampshire* was mined off the Orkneys when he was on his way to Russia, Lloyd George, after some hesitation, took on that role as well.

By now Asquith was losing the confidence of many of his own party, and the strain of the war was obviously telling on him. He still managed to have occasional games of chess and bridge at No. 10, and

Margot managed, also, to do some entertaining. But Asquith was drinking heavily and a change had to come. In December 1916 Margot's prediction that 'it is only a question of time when we shall have to leave Downing Street' came true, and, she recalled later, they left No. 10 with nowhere else to go. Lady Cunard, who was renting their house in Cavendish Square, let them use part of it until they could make permanent arrangements.

Lady Olwen Carey Evans, one of Lloyd George's five children, was twenty-four when the family moved into No. 10. Since she already lived next door at No. 11 she of course knew about developments in No. 10, and she recalls being reproved by her mother one day for remarking about Asquith 'not knowing what was going on, because he had drunk too much and had fallen asleep'. 'Mother was quite sharp as she reminded me that things seen and heard about my Father's Cabinet colleagues were not to be repeated – ever!' Lady Olwen wrote many years later.

The household that settled down in No. 10 for the rest of the war years, and for some years afterwards, was a lively, intense and dramatic one. It was full of contradictions: the whirling power house of the Prime Minister's personality; the placid motherliness of his wife, Dame Margaret; his lively sons and daughters; the enigmatic figure of his mistress, Frances Stevenson; and the endless comings and goings of politicians and officials. 'I loved living at No. 10,' Lady Olwen recalls, 'for there was always something going on. Famous people came and went, and No. 10 seemed to be the hub of the universe.'

There was much entertaining, and Dame Margaret coped easily and well. Lloyd George would send the people he had been meeting to tell her they were coming to lunch. General Smuts, the great South African leader, was among them. 'Your husband has sent me to tell you they are coming up, and there will be three of them.' Once, some years later, this easy hospitality nearly caused considerable embarrassment, but the moment was saved by the use of Welsh, which was often spoken in the Lloyd George household. Herbert Samuel, who was a very strict Jew, had been with Lloyd George, and was strongly pressed to stay for lunch. Dame Margaret, to her husband's astonishment, was obviously reluctant. She managed, eventually, to whisper to her husband, in Welsh: 'It's pork for lunch,' and so the invitation was gently turned into 'some other time'.

Dame Margaret managed, after some years of practice, simply to ignore the presence in the house of her husband's mistress. Frances Stevenson had originally been brought into the family to give extra tuition to Olwen's sister, Megan, and then had stayed on to go to No. 11 as Lloyd George's secretary. 'As far as the family was concerned, she was just another employee and we never discussed her,' Lady Olwen recalls. 'Mother certainly never mentioned her, but she quickly realised what was going on.' Certainly there was no love lost between Frances and the family. 'She spread lies about my supposed extravagance when I was first married, and tales about men friends of Megan's,' says Lady Olwen. 'She interfered with personal family files which my father kept in his office, and influenced him over money matters.'

For her part, Frances bitterly accused Dame Margaret of meanness and of deliberately making life uncomfortable for her husband. In her diary for 4 April 1915 she wrote: 'She [Dame Margaret] always wakes up when it is a question of money. As someone once put it, "As far as she is concerned, she would rather go without food than pay for it."' In 1917, soon after the family had moved into No. 10, she wrote:

D. has been very unhappy this week owing to the change from No. 11 to No. 10. They did not bother to get a comfortable room ready for him & the first night he came down to my office to work after dinner. The second night he did not come up to dinner at all as he & Mrs Ll.G. were not on speaking terms. She had closed the bedroom windows on the quiet, thinking that the room was cold, but knowing that he always gets a headache when he sleeps with closed windows ... She does not study him in the least – has hung up some hideous family portraits painted by some cheap artist, though he had had them taken down more than once before. In fact, the whole house is hideously uncomfortable at the present moment, quite unworthy of a Prime Minister & very irritating to him, for he has a keen sense of what is beautiful & artistic & what is not.

Frances Stevenson in her office in Whitehall

Lady Olwen's memories are very different. They are of her mother making No. 10 into a cosy family home, with their friendly Welsh servants around them, and rare but happy family times around the fire. Sometimes Dame Margaret, with her housewife's eye for economy, kept that fire too small, and there was a row when Lloyd George came home and found it down too low.

Frances noted these domestic events sharply: 'I have never seen anyone with such a capacity for making a place uncomfortable as Mrs Lloyd George', she wrote in her diary. 'Her meanness forces the household to economise in coal & food and everything that makes for comfort. The servants would be a disgrace to any house, & the PM is rightly ashamed of them.' Once again the memory of Lloyd George's daughter is very different. Lady Olwen remembers with great affection their housekeeper, Sarah Jones, whom they all called Lallie and who had come to No. 10 from the family home in north Wales. 'When people came to London from the constituency,' Lady Olwen remembers, 'they didn't come to see Buckingham Palace or the Tower of London, they came to see Sarah Jones. They used just to turn up at No. 10, and then they used to have great parties downstairs.'

Although there were searchlights and anti-aircraft guns in the Whitehall area, bombs fell alarmingly near No. 10 when the Zeppelin raids on London began. Lady Olwen and her father were alone in the house one night when they heard a crash. They both rushed out of their rooms and met on the landing. In their night clothes, they went down the staircase and out of the front door. On that occasion the Zeppelin dropped bombs on Piccadilly and in Camberwell, and if it was looking for the Houses of Parliament it did not find them. 'We were still looking up like a couple of fools,' recalls Lady Olwen, 'and the policeman said, "Don't you think you ought to go in now, sir?" So we did.'

Lady Olwen was then expecting a child. She had been married from No. 10 in June 1917 to a young army captain, Tom Carey Evans.

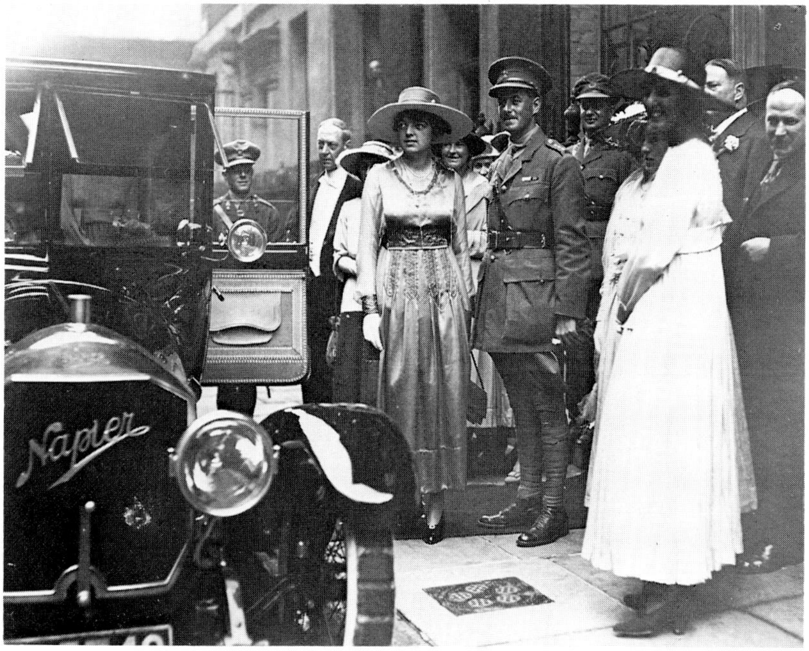

The wedding of Captain Tom Carey Evans and Miss Olwen Lloyd George, 19 June 1917

'Father', she wrote later, 'took a couple of hours off to give me away. There was a Cabinet meeting that morning, and apparently he looked at his watch and told his colleagues: "I'm sorry, but we will have to end the meeting here. I have an important engagement this afternoon."' The wedding was at the Welsh Baptist Chapel in Castle Street, and the reception was in the state rooms at No. 10. A multi-tiered wedding cake took pride of place and, during that period of wartime shortages, drew the envious eye of a guest who had recently been married, but without an iced cake. Obviously the cake resulted from the privilege of being the Prime Minister's daughter. But it was an elaborate fake made out of white cardboard, complete with decorations and a miniature bride and groom on top.

His grandchildren were a constant delight to Lloyd George. A.J. Sylvester, who was the Prime Minister's personal secretary from 1916 to 1945, recalls going into the Cabinet Room and finding him, with his back to the fireplace, watching with enormous delight as two of his tiny granddaughters ran round and round the top of the Cabinet table. 'L.G. was encouraging them,' Mr Sylvester remembers more than half a century later, 'he was laughing his head off, and full of joy.'

As the war went on, No. 10 expanded more and more to deal with it. Wooden huts were built in the garden as Lloyd George took over the control of affairs himself. He had a four-man War Cabinet, and went as seldom as he could to the Commons. He had, he said, too much work to do at No. 10. So the 'Garden Suburb', as it was called, grew and grew. In the end these huts, which spread over into St James's Park, housed more than 100 people, with a staff of fourteen charwomen to clear up after them.

When victory finally came Lloyd George's reputation was at its zenith. News of the armistice arrived, on 11 November 1918, when the Prime Minister was in bed, but he and then the whole household were roused with details of the wonderful victory. Crowds gathered in Downing Street, shouting for their hero, and Lloyd George went, triumphantly, to wave to them from an upstairs window.

But, as they were to be with Churchill nearly thirty years later, the crowds were fickle when the euphoria of peace was forgotten. Once again the Irish problem was proving to be beyond solution. In the early 1920s when the Black and Tan troubles broke out, massive barriers of wood, ten feet high, were erected across the end of Downing Street for fear of reprisals against the Prime Minister. At a general election immediately after the Armistice, Lloyd George had scored a personal triumph, but the Conservatives had a heavy majority in the new House and the Liberals were reduced to thirty-three. He struggled on in coalition, with an increasingly disaffected House of Commons constantly sniping at him, and in 1921 at last achieved an Irish settlement, which involved the retention of Ulster as part of the United Kingdom. To many diehard Conservatives it was a betrayal, and the newspapers, which had once lauded Lloyd George as the great national hero, increasingly turned against him. 'The Barnum of Downing Street' had lost his touch, and on 19 October 1922, at a crucial meeting at the Carlton Club, the Conservatives decided to leave the coalition. Lloyd

Lloyd George supervises the move out of No. 10

Barricades shut off the end of Downing Street from Whitehall as a protection against Irish demonstrators, December 1920

Lloyd George with Dame Margaret and their daughter Megan, on the day after his resignation, 28 October 1922

George said goodbye to his staff in the Cabinet Room, and he and his family, after six years of national and domestic drama, moved out of No. 10.

After Lloyd George's enormous vigour and zest for life, No. 10 now became a place of hushed quiet, and had about it, with every justification, the atmosphere of the sick-room. The new Prime Minister, Andrew Bonar Law, at the head of a Conservative Government with an overall majority of seventy-four, was a very sick and a very lonely man. He was sixty-four, a widower with two of his four sons killed in the war. Already suffering from cancer of the throat, he managed to struggle on despite his very considerable pain. His married elder daughter, Isabel, acted as his hostess – the christening party for her baby was in No. 10 – and he was well enough to entertain Mussolini to lunch in the State Dining-room during a conference of European Prime Ministers in December 1922.

Mussolini leaving No. 10 after lunching with Bonar Law, December 1922

The throat cancer, however, got worse and worse. Stanley Baldwin had to speak for him in the House of Commons, and in May 1923 Bonar Law resigned; he left No. 10 less than seven months after he had first moved in, and died on 30 October. The next two tenants of No. 10, Baldwin and Ramsay MacDonald, were among the pallbearers at his funeral in Westminster Abbey.

Baldwin was to be at No. 10 for almost as brief a spell as Bonar Law, although he was to return again twice, for substantial terms in office. On the steps of No. 10 he asked the well-wishers for their prayers rather than for their congratulations, but when he asked the electors for their support they refused to give it to him. The Conservatives lost

Andrew Bonar Law at his desk at No. 10, November 1922

eighty-eight seats at the election after the dissolution in November 1923, and in January 1924 Ramsay MacDonald went to the Palace to kiss hands with the King and so become Britain's first Labour Prime Minister. 'I had an hour's talk with him,' George V noted in his diary; 'he impressed me very much; he wishes to do the right thing'.

The 'right thing' included wearing formal court dress, a very elaborate and very expensive item. Many of his Labour colleagues felt MacDonald should not give in to such class-ridden formalities, but he retorted that it was the man, not his clothes, which mattered, and that it was pointless to start by giving offence. Eventually he was given his court dress by a member of the House of Lords.

Downing Street was now reasonably well furnished, but it completely lacked linen, china, glass and all the other details which were necessary for a home. MacDonald was a widower and his eldest daughter Ishbel was given the formidable task of running No. 10. Mrs Baldwin showed her round, and then Ishbel went off with the little money she had to buy what she needed. She went to the January sales, and bought things second-hand when she could. She realised she had to find enough not only for her family – there were three sisters and two brothers, although they were not all at home – but enough, too, for official entertaining. There was also the problem of staff, since the family were not used to servants. People from Lossiemouth, MacDonald's Scottish home, were found, and the family and their friendly servants settled down well.

The youngest of the daughters, now Mrs Sheila Lochhead, was thirteen when they first moved into No. 10. It was, she recalls, a 'completely unfamily house', with no private sitting-room for the people who lived there, and their bedrooms scattered around the rambling building. But when they settled down they thoroughly enjoyed themselves. Sheila's pocket-money was doubled from 3d. to 6d., in spite of her father's horror at the amount of money that had had to be spent on putting the place in livable order, and she amused herself practising, with one of the porters, her golf chip shots down the long corridor that leads to the Cabinet Room. 'There was that sort of atmosphere in the place,' she said. 'It was very nice.' And when golf practice got tedious there was always the magnificent set of banisters to slide down with the excuse that she was learning the Prime Ministers of England from their portraits on the walls as she whizzed past. Other portraits, too, were brought into No. 10 by MacDonald. He found that the walls of the house were generally bare, so he started the tradition that still exists of hanging pictures from the national galleries and museums.

As young Sheila was up in her room struggling with her homework, the Cabinet was making history a couple of floors below. She speculated on the possibility of hiding on the top of the bookcases and listening, but then she guessed they would be dusty, and that she might sneeze. 'I don't know how my father would have reacted.' The number of bookcases had to be increased in her father's day because MacDonald found it astonishing that there was no proper library at No. 10. He established the tradition of Cabinet ministers donating books to the house, and round the walls of the Cabinet Room created what became known as the Prime Minister's library. Between the bookcases there

Ramsay MacDonald leaving No. 10 for Buckingham Palace, to tender his resignation, November 1924

were racks of maps which ministers could pull out, like blinds, when they were discussing world problems. In the modern Cabinet Room, all but two of the bookcases have disappeared in order to make the room look lighter and less overpowering.

MacDonald's first stay in No. 10 lasted about ten months. Divisions in the Labour Party and a combination of Conservative and Liberal votes produced a massive defeat in the Commons in October 1924, and Baldwin returned to Downing Street as Prime Minister. With appalling industrial problems to deal with, by the spring of 1926 the Cabinet was meeting far into the night at No. 10. Baldwin presided with imperturbable calm, pipe firmly clenched between his teeth; it was said that, after Lloyd George's premiership, it was like a change from a man suffering from St Vitus' dance to a man suffering from sleeping sickness. Yet his movements were always brisk, sprinting up the stairs at No. 10 two at a time, leaping in and out of armchairs and sofas. He disliked the social life of the house, avoiding, when he could, such functions as a concert given by a White Russian Cossack choir in the garden of No. 10, with the singers using the Cabinet Room as their dressing-room.

The crisis of the General Strike, although it collapsed within days, left Baldwin exposed to the accusation of some of his party that he was too sympathetic to the unions. The trade depression, and the unemployment that went with it, seemed as insoluble as ever, and Baldwin turned his face firmly against demands for protection through

Cameras at No. 10 for the Labour Cabinet, 10 June 1929

The Derby Cabinet of 1867 in the Cabinet Room, by Henry Gales. The Prime Minister stands by the table on the right. Disraeli, the Chancellor of the Exchequer, stands on the left, holding a document

Above: Mr Gladstone's first Cabinet, 1868, in the Cabinet Room, by H. Barraud. No. 10 was at that time being used only as offices and for official entertaining
Left: W. E. Gladstone, 1879, by J. E. Millais

Right: Benjamin Disraeli, 1881, by J. E. Millais

The interior of No. 10 in 1907, by Charles E. Flower. *Above:* The Pillared Drawing-room. *Right:* The State Dining-room. *Opposite Top:* The Cabinet Room

Below: Two views of the gardens at No. 10, painted in 1888 by Philip Norman

Above: A. J. Balfour, by Philip de Laszlo
Above right: H. H. Asquith, 1919, by André Cluysenaar
Right: David Lloyd George, 1927, by William Orpen

Above left: Stanley Baldwin, *c.* 1933, by R. G. Eves
Above: Ramsay MacDonald, 1931, by John Lavery
Left: Neville Chamberlain, *c.* 1939, by Henry Lamb

Seascape, by Winston Churchill, which hangs in the White Drawing-room at No. 10

Winston Churchill, 'Blood, Sweat and Tears', by Frank O. Salisbury. The portrait hangs in the ante-room to the Cabinet Room

Ramsay MacDonald takes an early-morning walk in St James's Park with his son and daughter Alister and Sheila, and her pet, Scottie, October 1933

tariff reform. In 1928 his administration was responsible for giving all women the vote, on the same terms as men – a move that was rewarded in the general election of 1929 by many women voting against him, and with Labour becoming the largest party in the Commons.

Once again the Baldwins and the MacDonalds moved their china and glass and cutlery and private belongings in and out of No. 10. This time the MacDonald girls knew what to expect. Ishbel put pressure on the Office of Works to make the place more attractive, and Sheila had, like residents of No. 10 before and since, got used to London taxi-drivers not knowing where Downing Street was and taking her to the wrong address. There were pleasant social evenings – and an especial one when the television pioneer John Logie Baird came, with his elaborate equipment, to the Pillared Drawing-room.

Sheila was quite capable of coping with a domestic crisis when it occurred, even at the grandest event. On one occasion she had organised a formal luncheon party for her father in the State Dining-room. The food was still cooked in the massive kitchens down below, and was sent up to the dining-room in a small lift. Sheila ordered fish fillets for one course, but the worried parlourmaid found there were not enough, so she had to hurry to the sideboard and carefully cut the pieces in half. When the young Miss MacDonald was told about this small disaster, she investigated and found that the lift had been sent up from the kitchen to the dining-room with such gusto that the fish had shot off the dish and stuck to the roof of the compartment. As she says now, looking back on this domestic drama: 'Talk about flying fish ...'

Labour refused to accept the draconian economic measures – including a cut in the dole – that MacDonald thought were necessary to solve the great financial crisis of 1931. They refused also to accept the idea of, or to serve in, a coalition government. On Monday 24 August the King called all three party leaders together at Buckingham Palace, and they agreed to form a National Government. Only three members of the Labour Cabinet were prepared to continue, and at a tense, but fairly brief meeting in the Cabinet Room the second Labour Government came to an end.

The air of crisis had spread outside the walls of No. 10. Sheila MacDonald went up on to the roof – a favourite vantage point of generations of sons and daughters of Prime Ministers – and watched the urgent comings and goings as the National Government was formed. The country approved of the arrangement, even if the Labour Party did not, and in an autumn election the National Government won the vast majority of the seats. MacDonald remained at No. 10 until the summer of 1935. He had had an eye operation, and was exhausted by the strains of office, and deeply distressed by the vituperation which the Labour party had heaped upon him.

When the time came for him to retire [says Mrs Lochhead], I think he was really very glad. He had never really been happy in the National Government. He had really been heartbroken by the break with the Labour Party. When the time came for him to go home to Hampstead and to Lossiemouth he was really very relieved. He had been a sick man for several years; he should not have stayed on for so long, but he just kept on

The National Government, 1931. Ramsay MacDonald leads members of his Cabinet down the steps to the garden of No. 10. Behind him are J. H. Thomas, Lord Reading, Stanley Baldwin, Philip Snowden (with sticks), and (*top, right to left*) Lord Sankey, Sir Philip Cunliffe-Lister, Sir Samuel Hoare, Neville Chamberlain and Sir Herbert Samuel

thinking: Maybe I can contribute something. But I think he was glad to go ... I think there were two things he never recovered from in all his life: one was the death of my mother and the other was the break with the Labour Party.

Baldwin, who had been Lord President of the Council (a formal post with duties that can be as heavy or as light as the Prime Minister of the day wishes), changed places with MacDonald yet again, moving back to Downing Street in the summer of 1935. There he had to face the biggest crisis of his long career. There was already gossip, so far unreported in the British press, about the private life of the Prince of Wales. King George V died in January 1936, and the gossip grew as the new King continued his affair with the American divorcee, Mrs Wallis Simpson. Matters came to a head after a veiled reference to this affair by the Bishop of Bradford, and the English newspapers broke their silence. Parliament, the general public and the Commonwealth were opposed to such a marriage, and they were opposed, too, to the King's suggestion of a morganatic marriage. As the crisis grew, the new King came secretly to No. 10 to have urgent talks with the Prime Minister. Miss Sheila Minto, then a new young secretary working in the famous Garden Rooms that overlooked the rear entrance to No. 10, remembers the visits. 'We realised there was something afoot, and presently it became quite clear that the whole legal aspect of the affair

Mr and Mrs Baldwin leave No. 10 for the last time, 28 May 1937. 'I am a gentleman at large now,' he said

was being discussed,' she says. The office keeper at No. 10, a man named Carter, went down himself to open the door for the King, and then, sometimes accompanied by his brother, the future George VI, they walked along the garden path, in through the door, and up the stairs to the Prime Minister's office. 'Edward', recalls Miss Minto from those days when all the intensely interested secretaries had peered through their windows at these dramatic comings and goings, 'looked exactly like his photographs – small with a nice face. His brother George looked rather nervous and apprehensive. Edward VIII didn't look nervous; he knew what he was going to do or not going to do.'

For Baldwin, the successful handling of this major constitutional crisis was the final and greatest achievement of his long career. His quiet style, which had earned him a reputation of inactivity, was precisely what was needed for such a delicate matter, and after the Abdication, and the Coronation of George VI in 1937, he was able to retire in a glow of grateful recognition from the country. His reputation did not last, but his brilliant handling of the abdication crisis had undoubtedly helped to save the monarchy.

Except for the Churchills, the Baldwins were the last family to live in the state rooms at No. 10. When Neville Chamberlain became Prime Minister in 1937, he and his wife decided to stay at No. 11 (he had been Chancellor of the Exchequer under Baldwin) until some drastic changes had been made next door. Mrs Chamberlain decided that the state rooms were not practical any longer for private use, so rooms on the floor above, which for generations had been used as servants' quarters, were adapted for a private residence. Under the guidance of Sir Philip Sassoon, the immensely wealthy art connoisseur, the state rooms were completely redecorated, and antique furniture and pictures from the National Gallery were brought into them. The staircase was recarpeted in deep red with the walls repainted in a shade of green, and Mrs Chamberlain used a good deal of floral-patterned chintz for curtains and upholstery. The enormous kitchens, with the 16-foot-long kitchen table, massive butcher's block and rows of copper pots stamped 'V.R.', were modernised, and by the time the Chamberlains walked through the connecting door from No. 11 to their new home, some £25,000 had been spent on it.

Mrs Chamberlain leaves for the state opening of Parliament, 1938

Like Lloyd George and MacDonald before him, Chamberlain enjoyed walking in St James's Park before settling down to a day's work. A detective hovered nearby, but otherwise nobody took any notice. Mrs Chamberlain gave regular tea and sherry parties, but as the international political crisis grew, her husband had less and less time, and little inclination, to join them.

The atmosphere throughout No. 10 was growing increasingly tense as Hitler's ruthless ambitions became more and more apparent. The Cabinet met in constant and lengthy sessions, and Chamberlain flew three times to Germany to try to negotiate with Hitler, and so gain time for Britain to prepare for war. On the third occasion, when he flew to meet Hitler at Munich in September 1938, he was accompanied by his Parliamentary Private Secretary, Lord Dunglass, who was himself to become Prime Minister as Sir Alec Douglas-Home, and is now Lord Home of the Hersel. 'There was', Lord Home recalls, 'tremendous tension in No. 10, but of course we were so busy, with so many people from inside and outside the country all the time, that our noses were kept pretty well to the grindstone.'

When Chamberlain arrived back at the airport after his final meeting with Hitler, he deliberately waved the piece of paper, signed by Hitler, which said that future disputes between Britain and Germany would be settled by negotiation and not by force. Chamberlain thought that if this agreement was publicised and was then broken by Hitler, it would make it obvious to the world what kind of man the Fuehrer really was. When the Prime Minister got back to Downing Street, enormous crowds cheered him as he went through the famous door. Inside, the house was full of excited people, hoping against hope that the Prime Minister had averted war. They swarmed round him through the entrance-hall, along the long corridor towards the Cabinet Room, and up the newly carpeted staircase. Lord Home was a few paces behind him, and he heard somebody say – he does not know who it was – 'Neville, go to the window and repeat the historic statement "Peace with honour" ' – the phrase used by Disraeli to the Downing Street crowds when he returned triumphantly from the Congress of

'Peace in our time.' Chamberlain makes the fateful announcement from the window of No. 10, 30 September 1938

Berlin in 1878. Chamberlain turned, rather snappily, on whoever it was who made the suggestion and said, 'I don't do things of that kind.' But somebody else persuaded him: 'Oh, go on; get it done' – and he went, much against his better judgment, and called 'Peace in our time' to the delighted crowd. 'He knew it was a mistake and was fatal,' said Lord Home. ' "Peace in our time" was a great error of judgment, and he knew it.'

The Munich meeting had, at least, bought some time to prepare for war, and it came a year later when Hitler invaded Poland. Chamberlain

3 September 1939. Neville Chamberlain leaves No. 10 after making the broadcast declaring war with Germany. With him is his Parliamentary Private Secretary, Lord Dunglass, who later became Prime Minister as Sir Alec Douglas-Home

George VI visits the Prime Minister at No. 10 shortly before the outbreak of the Second World War

used the Cabinet Room as his office, and his Cabinet colleagues came and went there in constant procession, as an ultimatum was sent to Hitler on 2 September 1939. With the help of a Private Secretary, Chamberlain drew up the text of the broadcast he was to make from the Cabinet Room, on Sunday morning, 3 September; as Hitler had not responded to the ultimatum, the country was at war. Lord Home was in the Private Secretary's room next to the Cabinet Room, as the broadcast was being made, listening through the door as the Prime Minister spoke. It was, he thinks, the 'kind of message that people felt they wanted to hear from a Prime Minister who had tried all he could to gain peace, but had failed'. Once the broadcast was over, he recalls, the tension seemed to relax. 'When the decision had been taken, there was almost a feeling of relief. He had then to turn his attention to the conducting of the war.'

Chamberlain formed a War Cabinet, and brought in Churchill as First Lord of the Admiralty. But the Prime Minister was becoming more and more ill with the strain, and after the German invasion of Norway (which was as much Churchill's fault as Chamberlain's), he was obviously losing the confidence of his own party. In the vote on the Norwegian campaign the Government majority was drastically reduced, from 240 to 81. Clearly Chamberlain had to go. 'There was', says Lord Home, 'only one successor. Churchill had trained himself for war all his life. He used to deploy soldiers even when he was a child on the nursery floor. So he really knew the war game backwards.'

Churchill went to No. 10 on 10 May 1940, and there he and Lord Halifax sat in the Cabinet Room with Chamberlain, who told them that the Labour leaders would not work under him, so he had been unable to form a National Government. Later that day, after he had been to see the King, Churchill formed his Coalition Government, with a War Cabinet of five, including Chamberlain as Lord President of the Council.

Churchill urged the Chamberlains to stay on in No. 10 until the former Prime Minister had recovered his health. Finally, in the summer of 1940, the Churchills moved in. Chamberlain resigned because of ill-health at the beginning of October, and died of cancer on 9 November.

CHAPTER TEN

War and Peace

Churchill's immense personality is still, forty years after the end of the Second World War, tangibly present in 10 Downing Street. Every Prime Minister since his day has been well aware that he or she is sitting in Churchill's seat in the Cabinet Room; staff at No. 10 who were children – or perhaps not even born – when he was at the height of his power speak of him with awe; it is his portrait on the staircase, in its place with his forty-seven predecessors and successors, which immediately catches the eye; a large painting of him broods over the country's most senior statesmen as they gather outside the Cabinet Room for their regular meetings.

Yet Churchill in the peak of his career was to make rather less use of No. 10 than most prime ministers this century. It soon became evident, once the phoney war was over and the German bombing of London had begun, that the rickety old house was in absolutely no condition to offer much protection to the Prime Minister and his staff. Much sturdier accommodation was fitted up for him a few hundred yards away in the basement of a massively built government office block at Storey's Gate, and although Churchill went constantly back and forth to No. 10, it was at Storey's Gate that many of his greatest wartime decisions were made.

No. 10 in wartime
Top: Bomb damage in the state rooms
Middle left: The specially strengthened Garden Rooms
Bottom left: The War Cabinet in the garden of No. 10, 16 October 1941. Left to right, seated: Sir John Anderson, Winston Churchill, Clement Attlee, Anthony Eden; standing: Arthur Greenwood, Ernest Bevin, Lord Beaverbrook, Sir Kingsley Wood
Right: Workmen repairing damage in Downing Street caused by German bombs, October 1940

No. 10 was so obviously unsafe that it was decided to try to shore it up to withstand at least some of the danger from bombs. The ground-floor Garden Rooms were strengthened with massive beams, and the windows were covered with heavy steel shutters. It was here in spartan surroundings, in an atmosphere that became rather like the wardroom of a ship, that Churchill liked to entertain his wartime guests, and to discuss with them the policy that had to be pursued for winning the war. Mrs Churchill managed, with considerable skill, to make the rooms look reasonably comfortable, with fine glass and silver on the dining-table, and there she too would entertain the awe-struck mayors and council officials and war workers who had been invited to No. 10 as a reward for their war efforts.

King George VI was intensely interested in every aspect of the progress of the war, which he and his Prime Minister discussed over the dinner table in the Garden Rooms. These historic meetings are commemorated in a plaque which is in one of the rooms where the Garden Girls now pound their electric typewriters and word processors to cope with the endless correspondence of the present Prime Minister. The plaque says:

'In this room during the Second World War His Majesty the King was graciously pleased to dine on fourteen occasions with the Prime Minister Mr Churchill, the Deputy Prime Minister Mr Attlee, and some of their principal colleagues in the National Government and various High Commanders of the British and United States Forces. On two of these occasions the company was forced to withdraw into the neighbouring shelter by the air bombardment of the enemy.'

The 'neighbouring shelter' was a cramped, uncomfortable place, which Churchill – and everyone else in Downing Street – much disliked and which he would only rarely use. There was one occasion when John Peck (now Sir John), who was a Private Secretary, had to use all his tremendous authority as the Downing Street Air Raid Warden to order Churchill to the shelter! Churchill had heard the sirens go, and was told to go to the shelter. 'I'm not going,' he retorted. 'I'm sorry, sir, I'm in command here,' replied the fearless young Private Secretary. 'You really must go. All the rest of us have got to go in.' Churchill, rather amused but still grumbling, eventually went. But when nothing happened he announced that 'this is ridiculous', and stumped out – with the rest of the staff following him.

No. 10 was, however, quite severely damaged by bombs – and wartime photographs, which were not published at the time since they would have been useful propaganda for the Germans, show the house

Mrs Churchill in the White Drawing-room – the Boudoir. The photograph is by Cecil Beaton, and the portrait of Churchill by William Orpen

George VI and Queen Elizabeth leave No. 10 after lunching there with Churchill in 1941

with all the front windows shattered, and fairly extensive damage in some of the rooms. Churchill himself recalled one raid in his account of the Second World War. He and his guests had been dining in the Garden Rooms with the steel shutters closed, and they could hear bombs dropping close by.

Suddenly [he wrote] I had a providential impulse. The kitchen of No. 10 Downing Street is lofty and spacious, and looks out through a large plate-glass window about twenty-five feet high. The butler and parlourmaid continued to serve the dinner with complete detachment, but I became acutely aware of this big window, behind which Mrs Landemare, the cook, and the kitchen-maid, never turning a hair, were at work. I got up abruptly, went into the kitchen, told the butler to put the dinner on the hot plate in the dining-room, and ordered the cook and the other servants into the shelter, such as it was. I had been seated again at table only about three minutes when a really loud crash, close at hand, and a violent shock showed that the house had been struck . . .

We went into the kitchen . . . The devastation was complete . . . the blast had smitten the large, tidy kitchen, with all its bright saucepans and crockery, into a heap of black dust and rubble. The big plate-glass window had been hurled into fragments and splinters across the room, and would of course have cut its occupants, if there had been any, to pieces. But my fortunate inspiration, which I might so easily have neglected, had come in the nick of time.

Churchill's daughter Mary (now Lady Soames) remembers that Mrs Landemare's main concern was that the bomb had ruined her soufflé!

On another occasion the bombing also brought out Churchill's more extravagant taste in dress. Sir John Peck remembers that when an air-raid warning went, it was the job of the Private Secretary on duty to ring the Air Ministry to find out what was happening. On one occasion, as he was standing by the phone waiting for a reply, he looked into a mirror in front of him and saw the 'extraordinary apparition' of Churchill walking down the stairs, dressed in an enormous quilted Chinese dressing-gown, with red and gold dragons writhing round it, his gas-mask knapsack slung over one shoulder, and his tin hat on his head. When Churchill saw Sir John's astonishment, he grinned broadly and said: 'John, conditions of total war do produce some most remarkable spectacles.'

For some members of the staff at No. 10 this tremendous personality could be overwhelming, and too much to cope with. Miss Sheila Minto remembers one evening going through the ante-room of the Cabinet Room, where she found a girl obviously much distressed and 'looking like death'. 'I can't go in; I can't go in,' said the poor girl. 'He terrifies me.' A Private Secretary put his head round the Cabinet Room door and called to Miss Minto 'for God's sake' to go in and cope. She snatched the notebook from the weeping girl and went into the Cabinet Room where Churchill demanded, first to know who she was, and then ordered her to sit at a typewriter opposite him at the Cabinet table. Then he began to dictate to her, straight on to the typewriter. 'He got some jolly queer typing,' recalls Miss Minto, 'but I was quite experienced, so it was all right.' Every so often Churchill rang a bell, and a Royal Marine messenger would come in to take the manuscript away for further copying. Churchill was often not easy to hear, but Miss Minto coped so well that she was from then on in regular demand by the Prime Minister when he dictated his speeches. Sometimes he would start work at ten o'clock at night and go on until two or three the next morning. Sometimes, if he decided to work in bed – and he very often did – he would poke his head out of the bedroom door and say, with a mischievous grin, 'I think I'll need two women tonight.' The Private Secretary on duty had to attend the Prime Minister as he went to bed. He would solemnly undress, scratch his back with a long-handled ivory brush, put on a small silk vest, and then climb into bed and start work on his boxes or other official business.

When the end of the war came the atmosphere in No. 10 was one of intense relief. Churchill made a triumphant broadcast from the Cabinet Room – he had prepared it sitting up in bed and dictating to his secretaries – and there was, Sir John recalls, 'a sense of triumph and relief in the victory, heavily tempered by deep foreboding about the future'. For Churchill those forebodings were entirely justified, for within a very few months he was to be out of Downing Street. The victory in May 1945 was followed swiftly by a general election – the first there had been for ten years – and by the end of July Labour had

Churchill makes his VE-Day broadcast from the Cabinet Room in No. 10, 3 p.m., Tuesday 8 May 1945

scored a massive victory. The Churchills moved out of No. 10 to a suite in Claridge's, and Clement Attlee moved in.

There was no need now, of course, to use the bomb-proof annexe at Storey's Gate, and the Attlees moved into No. 10 itself. They arranged for further adaptations to be done to the flat which had been carved out of the upper floor for the Chamberlains – it now had its own kitchen – and their son and three daughters either lived there with them or were frequent visitors. Attlee, in his imperturbable and monosyllabic way, settled down to lead his Cabinet in the massive task of post-war reconstruction. Like Churchill, he was able to make a victory broadcast when the Japanese surrendered – 'The last of our enemies is laid low' – but the economic enemies still defied the Government.

Lord Wilson of Rievaulx, who as Harold Wilson was in the Attlee Cabinet as President of the Board of Trade, recalls one symbolic economy that the pipe-smoking Attlee imposed on his fellow ministers. The price of cigarettes had gone up in the budget from 2s. 4d. to 3s. 4d. for 20 – an enormous increase. It was an attempt to cut down on the drain on precious dollars that tobacco imports were costing. Attlee decided that the Cabinet should give a lead to the nation and smoking was banned in the Cabinet Room. From then on, members of the Cabinet found various ingenious excuses to slip out of the room to have a quick cigarette or draw on their pipes.

Attlee had had his long wartime experience as Deputy Prime Minister to Churchill, so he was steeped in the system of Government. His Cabinet meetings were brisk and businesslike, and ministers who tended to be long-winded were quickly told to make up their minds. Outside politics his great interest, and great relaxation, was cricket. It was an interest which some of his staff played on to bring No. 10 more

Clement Attlee in the Cabinet Room, 1946

up to date. His press secretary, Francis Williams, suggested to him that a news-agency teleprinter should be installed in the house to keep everyone up to date with worldwide events. Attlee could not see the point. He read *The Times* every day and *The Observer* every Sunday, and that should be enough. The staff, however, persisted, and they came up with a bright idea: did the Prime Minister know that there was a new machine out that regularly told you the cricket scores? 'What a splendid idea,' said the Prime Minister, 'we better have it.' So the teleprinter was duly installed, and for years the staff of No. 10 always called it the 'cricket machine'.

The 1945 election had brought hundreds of new, young MPs to the Commons, and Attlee felt it his duty to get to know his own supporters. They were invited, a dozen or so at a time, for tea at No. 10. 'A nice little tea,' Mr James Callaghan, the future Labour Prime Minister and occupier of No. 10, recalls, 'cucumber sandwiches and so on. We would perch round quite informally, and Clem had had made up a huge volume of photographs of all the new members, and made acid comments.' When it came to Mr Callaghan's own picture, the Prime Minister uttered the one word 'filmstar' and turned over.

Attlee had four and a half years to get to know those bright young men before the election of February 1950. Labour's overall majority in the Commons then fell drastically to seven, and in the election of October 1951 Attlee lost office. The Conservatives had an overall majority of seventeen, and Churchill was, once again, back in No. 10.

In their second term of office the Churchills lived at No. 10 for three and a half years. Churchill was seventy-six, and Mrs Churchill viewed the prospect of returning to Downing Street with some foreboding. 'Winston may not want to retire, but *I* do!' she would say, but Lady Soames recalls that her father went back there 'like a bird returning to its nest'. He resumed his old habit of using the Cabinet Room as his office: 'It was a very convenient room,' says Lady Soames, 'and I think it harmonised with his thoughts and was very conducive to pondering.' He resumed his habit of working in bed, and getting up late in the morning after ploughing through a great deal of work, and strewing his papers over the bed and on to the floor.

When they moved back Mrs Churchill thought it sensible to live in the convenient private flat, but Winston wanted to move back into the whole house. He used the Coronation in 1953 as an excuse to get his way. There would have to be a good deal of entertaining, he argued, and so they should use all the rooms available. Work was carried out to make this possible, and Lady Churchill transformed the White Drawing-room once again into her boudoir.

Churchill's health, however, could not stand both the strain of office and of age. Three weeks after the Coronation he gave a dinner in the State Dining-room at No. 10 for the Italian Prime Minister de Gasperi, and towards the end of the evening he suffered a slight stroke. Realising he was ill his guests left tactfully early. He managed to preside at a Cabinet meeting the next day, but then he went to rest at Chartwell.

Churchill, in court dress, says farewell to the Queen after she had attended a dinner in his honour at No. 10, on the eve of his retirement, 4 April 1955

He doggedly pulled through the crisis, and was well enough to make a triumphant speech at the Conservative Party conference that October. By the spring of 1955, however, it was time for the 80-year-old Prime Minister to go. On 4 April the Queen and the Duke of Edinburgh went to dinner with the Churchills in the State Dining-room at No. 10. Fifty guests sat round the great table – members of his family, political colleagues, and old friends from the war years. The three party leaders were there, along with the Speaker of the House of Commons. Mrs Chamberlain was invited back to the house in which she had taken such a great interest. Churchill, without using a note, made a speech of welcome to the Queen and proposed the toast to her; a toast which, he recalled, as a young cavalry subaltern, he had much enjoyed drinking to her great great grandmother, Queen Victoria. And then Sir Winston bade his Royal guests farewell on the doorstep of No. 10. The next day, 5 April 1955, he resigned.

Churchill's successor at No. 10 was inevitable. Sir Anthony Eden was the Foreign Secretary, a post he had also held through the war years, and was very much Churchill's heir-apparent. His second wife, Clarissa, was Churchill's niece (she was the daughter of Winston's only brother John) and they had been married from No. 10 in August 1952. The Edens knew No. 10 well, of course, and Lady Eden (now the Countess of Avon) was delighted to be living there. 'I thought it was the nicest house in London,' she says. 'It was the nicest house you could possibly wish to live in.' She especially liked the state rooms, and had hopes of getting rid of the pre-war decorations and restoring them to their former appearance. She investigated the original designs that Soane had drawn up for his great State Dining-room, and had plans to restore the extraordinary colours of green and magenta. There was, however, one of the inevitable spending cutbacks, and her plans had to be dropped.

Anthony and Clarissa Eden in the garden of No. 10 with Mr and Mrs Churchill, on their wedding day in 1952

As the hostess at No. 10, it fell to Lady Avon to organise the dinners that her husband gave to visiting politicians – although, she recalls, she did not go to them herself. The presence of women at the table would, it was felt, hinder the important conversation of the men, so she had to stay in her 'harem'. At one historic dinner, which took place in the State Dining-room on 26 July 1956, the Prime Minister was entertaining the young King Feisal of Iraq and his Prime Minister Nuri es-Said when a telegram arrived announcing that Egypt had seized the Suez Canal. Sir Philip de Zulueta was the Private Secretary on duty that evening, and he had the task of giving the Foreign Office telegram to the Prime Minister. It was a very formal, white-tie occasion but, as Sir Philip recalls, the news 'rather spoilt the excellence of our dinner. Everybody had to have meetings all night afterwards. It was certainly a very dramatic moment.'

For Lady Avon, the frantic pace at No. 10 which followed the Suez takeover meant even more organising of meals for the stream of people who now flocked to the house. 'It was very tense,' she recalls, 'and also it was never-ending. It went on all through the night; private secretaries were rushing in and out of the bedroom with papers. Crises were developing every night. Meals were regularly three hours late. Nobody knew where they were going to be.' The American Secretary of State, John Foster Dulles, flew over from Washington, and was added to the endless list of people who had to be made welcome. Lady Avon was by no means satisfied with the standards of the official Government hospitality department, so on one occasion she brought in a private catering firm. She heard Dulles say to his neighbour at the dinner table: 'I bet you five pounds I can tell you exactly what every course is going to be.' 'I had great satisfaction,' she says, 'when he lost his bet.' No

Sir Anthony Eden and Mr John Foster Dulles, the American Secretary of State, at No. 10 during the Suez crisis, August 1956

Clement Attlee, 1946, by George Harcourt

Sir Anthony Eden, 1970, in his Chancellor's robes of the University of Birmingham, by Derek Hill

Harold Macmillan, 1980, by Bryan Organ. The portrait hangs on the landing at the top of the main staircase in No. 10

Sir Alec Douglas-Home, 1980, by Suzie Malin

The State Drawing-room after the restoration of 1960–3. *Top:* The White Drawing-room. *Above:* The Blue Drawing-room. *Left:* The Pillared Drawing-room

Edward Heath, 1972, by Derek Hill

Top right: The Blue Drawing-room, with Edward Heath's grand piano in the White Drawing-room beyond. The two paintings are by Claude
Right: The State Dining-room in 1972, after Edward Heath had had the walls lightened and British paintings hung. The two larger paintings are by Gainsborough and the smaller one is a Romney

James Callaghan, 1983, by Bryan Organ

Harold Wilson, 1974, by Ruskin Spear

Margaret Thatcher, 1984, in the Blue Drawing-room, by Rodrigo Moynihan

wonder Lady Avon told a meeting of women Conservatives that she sometimes felt 'as though the Suez Canal is flowing through my drawing-room'.

As the Suez crisis became so acute, Lady Avon used all her energies trying to make everything as easy as possible for her husband. His health was getting worse and worse, and there was increasing public anger at the decision to send British troops to Egypt. Lady Avon got some relaxation by planting the garden with lilies and roses – it is the one part of the house where wives have been able, over the years, to imprint their own tastes – and on one occasion she walked from the back entrance of No. 10 up to Trafalgar Square to listen to Aneurin Bevan addressing an anti-Suez rally. 'People all around me began to recognise me,' she remembers; 'they were all terribly friendly and nice, but I thought it was getting a bit awkward, so I trickled back again.'

The public outcry against the Suez policy grew and there were resignations from the Government. Eden's health became steadily worse, and in November he and his wife flew to Jamaica for a holiday, leaving R. A. Butler in charge. But when on 9 January 1957 Eden resigned his office, it was Harold Macmillan who took over.

Macmillan was Prime Minister from 1957 to 1963. It was a long stint in office, but he and his wife lived in No. 10 for only half that time. For years it had been becoming more and more obvious that drastic repairs would have to be done to the house if it was to continue both as the Prime Minister's home and the headquarters of the administration; these repairs proved to be so extensive that it was impossible for either the Prime Minister or his staff to be there while they were being carried out.

There had, of course, been the usual government committee looking into the whole problem of the repairs. Chaired by an eminent man of the arts, the Earl of Crawford and Balcarres, it proposed extensive work not only on No. 10 but on Nos. 11 and 12 and on the Old Treasury

Harold Macmillan in the Cabinet Room, January 1957

Building on the corner of Downing Street and Whitehall as well. Like so many other official plans this one got hopelessly out of hand. The original estimates were that the work would cost £1.25 million and take about eighteen months to complete. In the end it cost nearly £3 million and took three years. The Cabinet had suddenly decided that the work was to begin in August 1960, before the contractors had had time to prepare the site, and thorough investigation of the old buildings showed that they were in a much worse state than anyone had imagined. A team of ex-miners was sent down to reconstruct the foundations, and they found that the great logs on which the houses had been based had dried out and crumbled. The walls of No. 11 were six inches out of true; floors were rotten; apparently solid walls were held up only by the plaster covering them; woodwork was riddled with disease. Tanks of chemicals were set up on the Foreign Office Green, beside Downing Street, to cure the woodwork, but the repairs on some of the doors became so intricate that they cost two or three times the value of a new door.

Added to all this there were endless labour problems leading to fourteen different strikes. The employers tried to counter trouble with bonus schemes, which only made matters worse, and at one time all worked stopped for three months. In the end it was estimated that the

The rebuilding of Downing Street
Left: No. 10 under its protective awning and encased in scaffolding
Below: The Prime Minister's Christmas card for 1960, showing the Prime Minister and Lady Dorothy Macmillan in the garden of No. 10 during the rebuilding
Bottom: the corridor from the front door to the Cabinet Room

Sir Alec Douglas-Home leaving the Foreign Office for Buckingham Palace, to be invited to form a government

strikes cost nearly half a million pounds – something like a sixth of the total cost of the reconstruction. Eventually work was completed under the vast temporary roof that had been built across Downing Street – and the street itself had acquired a new house. No. 12 had been burnt down in 1879, but now it was rebuilt as the Government Whips' office. As for the rest of the buildings, it was estimated that about forty per cent were replicas or restorations of what had been there before, but sixty per cent of Downing Street was entirely new.

The newspapers, of course, were scandalised at this vast outpouring of public money, and they would have been further outraged if they had known that yet more would have to be spent within a few years to put right another list of problems with No. 10. After Macmillan's resignation in October 1963, Sir Alec Douglas-Home (having disclaimed his peerage) was Prime Minister for just under a year before Labour won the election of October 1964 and Harold Wilson moved into No. 10. But the Wilsons could do little entertaining because of the appearance of dry rot in the state rooms. There was dust everywhere, and dust sheets covered the furniture.

However, Lady Wilson did manage to get one of No. 10's traditional pieces of decoration restored. When she and her husband moved in they found that the portraits of the Prime Ministers had been taken down from the walls of the main staircase. When the Macmillans had moved back to No. 10 from Admiralty House, where they had been living while the repairs were carried out, Lady Dorothy Macmillan had decided that the portraits should be rehung in one of the corridors. 'That was fine for her,' says Lady Wilson, 'but I thought it would be nice to get them back on the stairs.' She persisted, against official lack of enthusiasm, and eventually got her way – to the great delight of

Right: Mr and Mrs Wilson with their two sons, Giles and Robin, and the family cat, Nemo, at No. 10

Below: On the doorstep of power. Harold Wilson, aged eight, poses for his father outside No. 10 when the family were visiting the Wembley Exhibition in 1924

today's visitors to No. 10, for the portraits are one of its most fascinating features.

Harold Wilson has been the only modern Prime Minister to use No. 10 only for official purposes, and to live with his wife in their own home. They lived in No. 10 during his first term of office, but after his re-election in 1974 they decided they would rather have a 'proper home' again. Late at night Lady Wilson found that the place, empty of people, could be rather lonely, while at other times it could be overfull. While the Wilsons were living there the doorkeeper once kept a check on the comings and goings through the famous front door, and he found that between 6 a.m. and 11 p.m. the front door of No. 10 was opened 945 times.

Lord Wilson is also the only Prime Minister who has reported seeing a ghost at No. 10. It was a lady dressed in pink whom he saw once in the private flat. She was there, too, one morning when a cleaner was busy dusting in the flat. 'Perhaps,' speculates Lady Wilson, 'she was left over from the days when it was a private house.'

In the years between the two Wilson administrations Edward Heath, Prime Minister from 1970 to 1974, finally managed to get No. 10 back to the general appearance it had in Walpole's day. He made a virtue out of necessity when more repairs had to be done because of the dry rot in the state rooms. He was able to have the rooms entirely redecorated in their original style, with the walls covered in figured silk. 'It is a splendid house with great traditions,' he says, 'but I thought it dowdy and seedy, and it really needed doing up properly.' He had poor-quality paintings replaced by works of great British and French

Mrs Wilson watches the arrival of President Nixon from an upstairs window at No. 10, February 1969. She later had letters of complaint from people who said her curiosity was bad manners

Left: Mr Heath's piano is moved into No. 10 from his flat in Albany, July 1970
Below: Edward Heath at No. 10, May 1973

Above: A happy James Callaghan arrives at No. 10, April 1976
Right: Summit at No. 10, 9 May 1977. President Jimmy Carter and Chancellor Helmut Schmidt with Mr Callaghan

artists; the State Dining-room had a new table and carpet, and the panelled walls were made much lighter. Pieces of fine furniture were brought in from museums to enhance the elegant rooms.

Mr Heath took great pride in extending the artistic life of the house. Like Balfour before him, he brought in his own piano; he organised concerts, and had grace sung by a choir before and after formal meals. He found the private flat the most unsatisfactory part of Downing Street because he thought it was badly designed, but the rest of the house he enjoyed enormously. 'The people who go there like the intimacy of No. 10,' he says. 'That is why I thought it necessary to get away from the old shoddy things and really have lovely things at No. 10. That is what I tried to provide.'

One of his successors at No. 10, James Callaghan, was much less impressed by the house. Unlike his wife, he did not very much enjoy living there. Audrey Callaghan found it a 'great experience' and something she would not have missed, but her husband would have preferred their home in Sussex. Yet, like every Prime Minister, Mr Callaghan was intensely aware of the historical values of the house. 'I genuinely felt I was a trustee of the past as well as the custodian of the present and, perhaps, the future,' he recalls. The Cabinet Room, above all, impressed him. 'Some great scenes in British history have been enacted in that room, and unless you are entirely deficient of a sense of history, it was rather tremendous to feel part of the moving pattern which I trust will go on for another 250 years yet.'

For the Callaghans that pattern changed in the early spring of 1979, when his government was defeated in the House of Commons by one vote. No. 10 was once again, in its centuries of history, to have a new tenant.

CHAPTER ELEVEN

The Lady of the House

The first woman tenant of 10 Downing Street moved in on 4 May 1979, 244 years after it had become the official home of the First Lord of the Treasury. Mrs Margaret Thatcher was not given the keys of the front door, since no Prime Minister is ever given them. There is no need. Policemen and doorkeepers are on duty all day every day, and no Prime Minister has ever had the indignity of fumbling for the keys of the famous front door before a crowd of interested onlookers.

It is a door which, with its elaborate wrought-iron archway in front, surmounted by a lantern topped by a crown, is always kept immaculately glossy and shiny. The letter-box, with its inscription 'First Lord of the Treasury', is polished every morning, and so is the brass door-knob below it. The lion-head door-knocker, once touched for luck by troops going off to the trenches in the First World War, is dusted and the steps kept immaculately clean. There are, in fact, two front doors for No. 10. One is kept in reserve ready for the time when the one in service needs repair or repainting. Then all the fittings are carefully switched over from one to the other.

Beyond that famous front door and its unimpressive exterior, 10 Downing Street is a political Tardis. Like Doctor Who's time machine the door opens on to a seemingly endless warren of corridors and staircases and rooms, and the whole confusing, rambling building is made even more complicated by the fact that the ground on which it is built slopes steeply, so that rooms at the back of the house which seem to be on the ground floor turn out to be actually on the first floor.

When the front door opens to admit famous visitors, the cameras sometimes get a quick glimpse of the hallway beyond. The black and white marble chequered floor, first put down in the eighteenth century, has been restored after Victorian attempts to make it more impressive with elaborately decorated tiles, and in one corner stands a magnificent Chippendale porter's chair, hooded and upholstered in dark leather, and a favourite place from which No. 10's formidable cat, Wilberforce, inspects the comings and goings. On the right of the entrance hall is a large marble fireplace, filled with elaborately arranged flowers, and here Mrs Thatcher stands to be photographed with her more important

Mrs Thatcher, with her husband, takes over at No. 10, 4 May 1979

visitors. A ten-foot-high long-case clock with steel and brass face, made by Benson of Whitehaven, ticks loudly against one wall. And eyeing the visitors from the wall opposite the front door are large portraits of Sir Robert Walpole himself and of the Earl of Chatham – a rather odd choice for such a prominent position since, although Chatham was Prime Minister, he never lived at No. 10.

Beyond the entrance-hall begin what seems to be acres of gold-coloured carpets which stretch down the endless corridors of the house, cover the floors in the ante-rooms and offices, and carry on up the confusing number of staircases. Once all this used to be a rather grand red, but the present colour is very much in keeping with Mrs Thatcher's taste. She dislikes heavy colours and decorations and approves of shades and patterns which give lightness and airiness to the house.

The carpet winds its way along the immense corridor that leads, eventually, to the Cabinet Room. On one side of the corridor there are high windows; on the other, portraits of actors and actresses – Ellen Terry, Garrick, Sarah Siddons – and beyond that a Henry Moore reclining figure in an alcove. Mrs Thatcher has arranged these as 'a little art gallery', and it is one of several groups of 'people of interest and achievers' that she has had brought into the house from galleries and museums.

In the ante-room of the Cabinet Room, Mrs Thatcher has made a small concession about the furniture and decorations of No. 10; she has allowed the brown baize to stay on the oval-ended table in the middle of the room. With her dislike of heavy colours, the brown-baize doors which were in No. 10 when she came there have been replaced with others of white-painted wood and glass that were resurrected from the basement, but she has allowed baize to stay on the ante-room table because this is the room where ministers gather, sometimes in rather nervous conversation, before Cabinet meetings. They invariably have their red boxes full of official papers, and dump them down unceremoniously on the table. Rather than let such a fine piece of furniture get scratched, the brown baize has stayed.

Brooding over the gathered ministers is a large portrait of Churchill entitled 'Blood, Sweat and Tears, 1942–3', by Frank O. Salisbury, and beside the double doors of the Cabinet Room itself – double so that the discussions cannot be listened to by inquisitive ears outside – there is a long-case clock, its chiming mechanism turned to 'silent'. On the left-hand side the cypher WIVR is carved into the wood, and below it Ind Bd (for India Board), indicating that it once kept time in another house in Downing Street, where the India Board had its offices.

Like so much else about No. 10, the Cabinet Room, the very centre of power and authority in Britain, is understated and undramatic. Without its immense historical connections it would seem simply a rather large, bright and well-proportioned room, lit by high windows. Its walls are painted off-white; three electric brass chandeliers hang from the high ceiling; and there are two large bookcases – all that are left of the ones that used to take up so much space in the room – along one wall. Many companies have boardrooms which are far more grand and expensively furnished and decorated; but none of them has, even remotely, the history this room contains.

Dominating the room, of course, is the Cabinet table – described tactfully as boat-shaped, less tactfully as coffin-shaped. It has a modern top on the original massive legs which support it. Mrs Thatcher is not enthusiastic, partly because it is covered with the dreaded brown baize, and partly because she would like to see the fine original oak table-top restored to its proper place. 'We must find it,' she says.

The original chairs still surround the table – the ones that the cabinets of Disraeli and Gladstone used, made of solid mahogany with scrolls carved into the backs. There are twenty-three of them round the table – one at the end is traditionally reserved for the Chief Whip, who is called into Cabinet meetings – each upholstered in tan-coloured hide. Only one chair has arms, the Prime Minister's, from which she presides at Cabinet Meetings, sitting half-way along one side of the table, in front of a fine marble fireplace and beneath the only picture in the room. That picture is, as it certainly must be in such a place, a portrait of 'Sir Robert Walpole K.C. The first Prime Minister to occupy 10 Downing Street, by van Loo'. In fact it is not the original portrait, which went to Russia when Walpole's pictures were sold after his death

Mr and Mrs Thatcher in the sitting-room of their private apartment at No. 10. All the furniture is Government-owned, as is the Lowry, but the Thatchers have brought their own family pictures and ornaments

The Cabinet Room (*top right*). The Prime Minister's chair (*top left*) is the only one with arms. Beyond the blotter are a silver William IV wafer box and a silver candlestick which once belonged to Pitt and Disraeli. The double doors in the Principal Private Secretary's office (*above*) lead to the Cabinet Room. The long-case clock outside the doors (*right*) was once in the India Office. It is by Samuel Whichcote of London

Left: Ministers gather in the Ante-room before a meeting. They include, from the left, Norman Fowler, Lord Young, John Selwyn Gummer, Sir Robert Armstrong, Norman Tebbit, Kenneth Baker and Lord Whitelaw
Below: The Prime Minister presides over a meeting in the Cabinet Room at No. 10. On her left is Lord Whitelaw and on her right Sir Robert Armstrong, the Cabinet Secretary. The portrait of Walpole, over the fireplace behind her, is the only picture in the room

The Prime Minister at work in her study (*below*). On the wall behind her (*and right*) is The River Party: The Rosoman Family, by Johan Zoffany, which used to hang in the Pillared Drawing-room

The Blue Drawing-room (*above*), where the Prime Minister receives her guests at formal receptions and dinners, also contains a George III commode (*right*) and a Chippendale card table (*far right*). Over the fireplace is a portrait of Peel, and beyond it one of Nelson. The other two pictures are by George Romney

Above: The White Drawing-room, traditionally the Boudoir for Prime Ministers' wives. The paintings are both by Turner

Below: Five Staffordshire figures in the White Drawing-room: (*left to right*) Wellington; Disraeli; Gladstone; Peel; Cobden

An Adam bombé commode in satinwood and walnut in the White Drawing-room

Above: The Pillared Drawing-room, the biggest of the state rooms. The paintings include, from the left, Master Newman and, over the fireplace, William Pitt, both by George Romney, and Master Smith by Francis Cotes. The Persian carpet (*top right*) is a copy of the original which is in the Victoria and Albert Museum

A Kent table and mirror (*above*) and a marble-topped Kent table (*right*) in the Pillared Drawing-room. Above it is a portrait of Sir William Fawcett by Joshua Reynolds

The State Dining-room. The chairs were originally in the British Embassy in Brazil. The portraits are of George II by John Shackleton (see page 40) and Sir Thomas Graves by James Northcote

Top right: A formal dinner to the Prime Minister of Canada in the State Dining-room

Right: The small dining-room with the State Dining-room beyond. The bust is of Sir Isaac Newton

Below: The ante-room to the state rooms. The furniture, by Thomas Chippendale, was made for Clive of India. On the table (*right*) is a bowl of dried lavender, brought by Mrs Thatcher from Chequers

The doorway (on the right) between No. 10 Downing Street and No. 11, where the Chancellor of the Exchequer has his official residence. The painting is a Vernet

Above: The front door of No. 10 from the entrance-hall, which contains the Chippendale hooded porter's chair (*right*) occupied by Wilberforce, No. 10's resident cat

Left: The main staircase at No. 10. Portraits of all British Prime Ministers, from Sir Robert Walpole to James Callaghan, line the walls. They are slightly rearranged after a new Prime Minister is appointed to make room for the previous holder of the office

Left: Downing Street today, and (*above*) the famous front door. The red-brick house at the end – No. 12 – was entirely rebuilt during the reconstruction in the 1960s. It is the office of the Government whips

The garden serves both Nos. 10 and 11 Downing Street

and is now in the Hermitage Museum in Leningrad. The Cabinet Room version is a copy, either by van Loo himself or by his studio.

In front of the Prime Minister's place at the table is a silver William IV wafer box, used now for pencils and pens, and beyond that a splendid silver candlestick, once owned by Pitt and then by Disraeli, and given to Macmillan in 1957 for the Cabinet Room. Two other pairs of silver candlesticks (a Georgian pair was given by Lord Avon) are precisely placed at even intervals along the table, and before each seat is a leather blotter, with cream blotting paper, stamped with the words 'Cabinet Room, First Lord', and with a crown and the royal cypher.

At one end of the Cabinet Room are two pairs of classical pillars, marking the place where the room was extended during one of the many alterations to the house. Beyond them are the two bookcases, with books given over the years by members of the Cabinet. Some are in imposing leather-bound sets; others are their own works – *The Regeneration of Britain* by Anthony Wedgwood Benn; *Aneurin Bevan* by Michael Foot; *The Body Politic* by Ian Gilmour. Who, one wonders, gave *God's Children with Tails* by Violet Campbell?

The Prime Minister's anti-baize campaign has not yet penetrated to the office of her Principal Private Secretary, just beyond the Cabinet Room. Once it was a waiting room next to 'My Lord's Study', but now it is the office for the most senior civil servant in No. 10. The baize – this time it is navy, not brown – has survived on a magnificent pair of double doors that lead into the Cabinet Room, and to one side of them is the Principal Private Secretary's desk, a marvel of Victorian mahogany solidity. A globe of the world stands in one corner, a reminder of the far-flung ramifications of the work done in this imposing room, and in the room beyond, where most of the other Private Secretaries have their desks, there is another reminder of the sudden dramas of international politics. Between the high windows of what the old plans show as 'My Lord's Dining Room' are three large brass ship's clocks, easily visible from each of the five heavy mahogany desks. The clock on the left shows the time in the United Kingdom; in the centre the time in Washington; the clock on the right usually shows the time in Moscow, but it can be changed to anywhere in the world when a crisis blows up.

Mrs Thatcher does most of her work in her study rather than in the Cabinet Room. Many of her predecessors, including Churchill, used the Cabinet Room as their private office, but she feels more comfortable in the room that was once the prime ministerial bedroom and bathroom. Not, however, until she had had some drastic changes made. 'I like things light,' she says, 'but when I first came here the walls of the study were covered with heavy sage-green damask-flock wallpaper. It was oppressive, but it looked as if it was going to last for another twenty years. So I had it re-done myself at my own cost.' Now the sun shines in on walls papered in pale grey strips, and on furniture upholstered in cream-coloured damask.

In one corner of the Prime Minister's study is a magnificent Queen Anne walnut bureau. She delights in showing it to visitors, and opening its mirrored doors to disclose more complicated doors and mirrors and drawers inside. Two small shelves pull out in front of the mirrors as stands for a pair of silver candlesticks, which then throw the reflected candlelight down on to the desk. Behind the Prime Minister's own desk is a Zoffany of the Rosoman family – it used to be in the Pillared Drawing-room – and on a wall in front of the chair in which she does much of her work is a portrait of the young Nelson, which she had brought to her office. He is one of the Prime Minister's heroes – she has had another portrait of him put in the Blue Drawing-room – and she likes to see him shown in his prime, as a young man without his eyepatch and the empty arm of his coat.

Like so much else in Downing Street, the bureau and the portrait and a great many other pictures, ornaments and furniture do not belong there. They come from various museums and galleries, and are simply there on loan. It sounds like a housewife's dream to be able to go round the nation's finest collections, selecting anything that takes the Prime Minister's eye. But it is not, apparently, at all like that. 'Oh, they will not let me have the best,' says the Prime Minister. 'They hide it when you go round!'

Only a few very important visitors get as far as the Prime Minister's study, or even – and these are the most important people of all – as far as the Cabinet Room for talks with the head of the Government. The great majority of people invited to No. 10 are entertained in the splendid formality of the state rooms. To get there they have to wind their way, sometimes in rather long and slow-moving queues, up the main staircase, and past the prints and photographs of all the other Prime Ministers on the wall. Only the last one, of Mr Callaghan, is in colour; all the rest are in black and white. As each Prime Minister departs from No. 10, the pictures are slightly rearranged to make room for the previous holder of the office at the very top of the stairs. Beyond the stairs there is a small landing, and the Prime Minister finally receives her guests in the Blue Drawing-room.

There are generally three large parties given every year at No. 10, to which people in all walks of life are invited. Groups of people with special achievements – exporters, for instance – are also invited to meet the Prime Minister, and there are endless lunches and dinners for visiting politicians. Since the rebuilding of the early 1960s these events are safely and smoothly run. Before the rebuilding, members of the staff had to be stationed between the rooms to make sure that the several hundred guests at the big events moved round and did not overload the decidedly unstable floors.

The impression guests receive when they first come into the state rooms is one of subdued and carefully restrained splendour. In the evening the massive crystal chandeliers glitter from the high ceilings, and show up the richness of the silk-covered walls. In the Blue Drawing-room two George II commodes stand between the windows, which are draped in swags of silk to match the walls. To one side of the large carved marble fireplace is the portrait of Nelson which Mrs

Thatcher had put there; on the other side is a portrait of the Duke of Wellington, who would himself have used the room when he lived at No. 10. In one corner is a battered, decidedly rickety desk, with a much-worn red-leather top, which is said to have been the one used by Pitt when he lived so uneconomically at No. 10. It is the only memory of his years there that still remains in the house; it is, in fact, one of the remarkably few pieces that have any connection with any of the former First Lords.

The White Drawing-room is the smallest of the state rooms, and the most attractive. It is small enough not to be overpowering or dauntingly formal, and to the staff it is still known as the Boudoir. In fact it was precisely that from the first years of No. 10: Lady Walpole used it as her boudoir; 200 years later Lady Churchill used the room in precisely the same way. Staffordshire figures of Gladstone, Beaconsfield and Wellington (all of whom lived in the house), and of Peel and Cobden (who did not), are on semi-circular side tables beside the marble fireplace, and an Adam commode in satinwood and walnut stands beneath a magnificently elaborate gilded mirror. Three Turner landscapes are on the walls, but rather hidden away in one corner is a seascape – the only picture in No. 10 by Churchill.

The most splendid – and altogether the most formal and intimidating – of the three reception rooms in the Pillared Drawing-room. The two pillars at one end had cleverly concealed steel supports inserted into them in the 1960s' rebuilding, and between them stands a heavily elaborate gilded and marble table by William Kent, the architect who remodelled the two houses for Walpole. On the floor, bearing the brunt of generations of shuffling feet, spilt drinks and trodden-in cocktail snacks, is a magnificent Persian carpet. It is a copy of a sixteenth-century carpet in the Victoria and Albert Museum, with an inscription woven into it which reads: 'I have no refuge in the world other than thy threshold. My head has no protection other than this porchway. The work of a slave of the holy place, Maqsud of Kashan in the year 926' (the Muslim date corresponding to 1520). A portrait of William Pitt by Romney gazes down on the guests from a large gilded frame above the fireplace, and on one of the gilded side tables are silver trophies won by the Earl of Bridgewater in 1809 for Five Best South Down Hogs!

Prime Ministers have always been fond of the small dining-room, and have used it both for their own family meals and for relaxed entertaining of important guests. Mrs Thatcher has used the room as a gallery of eminent British scientists. There is a bust of Isaac Newton, and pictures of Joseph Priestley, Humphry Davy and Edmund Halley (by Kneller). The mahogany dining-table has eight chairs round it, and if conversation should flag during meals the host can always get it going again by pointing out the very odd architectural feature of the room. Above the fireplace, where the chimney breast should be, there is, instead, a large window.

Beyond the small dining-room lies the State Dining-room, a room as impressive as its name implies. Soane's high, vaulted ceiling gives the place an air of ceremony and formality, and massive pieces of silver, brought to No. 10 since Mrs Thatcher moved in, gleam on the Adam mahogany sideboard and along the enormous dining-table. Some of the pieces are 'Speaker's Silver' – silver, that is, that Speakers once received for use in their own official house when they took office, and which they were allowed to keep as an extremely valuable perk when they retired. Regimented in absolute formality round the table are twenty reproduction Adam dining chairs, made originally for the British Embassy in Rio de Janeiro, but brought back to No. 10 after the Embassy moved to the ultra-modern Brasilia. And presiding over all this splendour is a vast portrait of George II, the man who first gave No. 10 to the First Lord of the Treasury.

From these grand rooms, visitors to No. 10 can get at least a glance at the garden which spreads behind it – and behind No. 11, without any barrier between the two. It is no longer 'fitted wth variety of Walle fruite & divers fruite Trees', as it was in Mrs Hampden's day, but there are still 'Plants, Rootes and flowers, very pleasant to the eye and profitable for use. Also severall handsom delightfull Gravelly Walkes, seats & arbors.' A large lawn now sweeps around the back of the two famous houses, and the 'Plants, Rootes and flowers' are in pleasantly laid-out rosebeds, with flowering and evergreen shrubs against the high old brick wall.

In the middle of the lawn there is a fine ilex tree, with seats under its shade, and tubs of flowers stand on the steps which lead down to the garden. Here, generations of Cabinets have sat in rows on the lawn to have their photographs taken, or strolled nonchalantly down the steps for the newsreel cameras. It is surprisingly large and delightfully quiet for a garden in the very centre of London. But it is as formal as a public park, and while visitors may certainly actually walk on the lawns, there is an atmosphere about the garden that makes you think that perhaps you ought not to.

Parties are occasionally held in the garden, but very few visitors indeed to No. 10 penetrate beyond these official and formal parts of the house to the private rooms, the apartments that the Chamberlains first had made, and which have been adapted and modernised for successive Prime Ministers. This is the part of No. 10 where Prime Ministers and their families can be alone and away from officialdom. Even here, of course, their staff can come to them when there is some important development, but it is here, also, that they can relax and become, even briefly, ordinary citizens.

Prime Ministers' wives have reacted very differently to the private flat. Lady Wilson found it sunless and cut off; Mrs Callaghan found it sunny and welcoming. Mrs Thatcher has made it very much her own – and with her enthusiasm for lightness she has turned the main bedroom into the sitting-room because, she thought, it was getting more sunlight. For the furniture in the sitting-room the Prime Minister has chosen two two-seater settees, covered in a floral pattern of red and

The Queen Mother leaves No. 10 after dining with the Prime Minister in the private apartments, November 1980

blue on a cream background. The cushions and curtains match, and so do the seats in the window recesses. Above one of the sofas is a Lowry townscape, 'Lancashire Fair, 1946', which used to be in the Prime Minister's study, but which Mrs Thatcher had moved to her living-room. Like everything else, it is Government-owned. 'It's much too expensive for us,' says the Prime Minister.

There are, of course, some private things around – 'Some of the bits and pieces are mine' – and there are family photographs on the side tables. A large plaque with a portrait of Mrs Thatcher, made of fine inlay work, was given to her when she signed the Hong Kong agreement in China in 1984. Large arrangements of flowers stand on the tables, and over the electric fire in the fireplace there is a drawing of a head of a woman by Henry Moore, and signed 'For Margaret Thatcher'.

Part of her own large collection of Derby and Staffordshire china, about which she is very knowledgeable, is in a recess by one of the windows. Much more of it is in big display cabinets in the passageway leading to the flat.

Mrs Thatcher describes it as a homely room. It is official furniture but 'it is *nice* official furniture', and she and Mr Thatcher can genuinely feel at home there. Yet they can never forget the world outside. However late the Prime Minister comes home from her long list of engagements, there are always red boxes to be gone through before she can go to bed. Officials can come here when there is something important she ought to be told about, so she is never really off duty. At weekends they try to get away. 'It's not very nice being here at weekends,' she says. 'Somehow the whole place is a morgue. It's so terribly quiet.'

The part of the private flat that does rather disappoint Mrs Thatcher, as a housewife, is the kitchen. And it most certainly is not grand, or remotely like the ideal kitchen of the colour supplements. She calls the long, narrow room, with its very ordinary blue and white fittings, a 'galley kitchen'. 'You can't eat in it,' she says. 'There isn't room for a table; I long for a really large kitchen where you can spend a lot of your time.' The Thatcher tastes, when they are at home, are for simple meals – shepherd's pie, lasagna and chicken pie, plus meals out of the deep-freeze which is stocked from a 'very well-known chain store'. Pencils stick out of a pot on one of the work surfaces, handy for Mrs Thatcher to leave notes about needing more coffee, or clear soup or pepper. No official domestic staff is provided, so the Prime Minister has made arrangements herself for two dailies to come in and keep the place immaculate.

When entertaining is done at home, and it is usually for very close personal and political friends, the meals are in the dining-room next to the kitchen. It has a table with six Hepplewhite chairs, each carved with the Prince of Wales feathers, and the food is served from a trolley with hotplates. There is a large Regency sideboard with an engraved glass goblet on it. On the goblet is etched a view of No. 10, and the rather mysterious inscription 'Queen Elizabeth 1575 Margaret Thatcher 1975'.

The private flat at No. 10 is the sort of place where a successful businessman might spend his working week before going off to his country home at weekends. Like the whole of No. 10, it entirely lacks the ritual grandeur with which some heads of government surround themselves. The old house has, as everyone who has lived or worked there invariably emphasises, somehow retained the atmosphere of a home. They feel very much that they belong to a close and immensely loyal group, and because No. 10 is relatively small, it means that the numbers who surround the Prime Minister must always be kept within bounds. There simply is no space there for the depredations of Parkinson's law to operate.

'This place seeps into your blood,' says Mrs Thatcher. 'It becomes part of your life. It is, above all, a home – and it is a house of history.'

OCCUPANTS OF NO. 10

Since No. 10 Downing Street was handed over to Sir Robert Walpole by George II in 1835, the following have lived there (PM = Prime Minister, FL = First Lord of the Treasury, CE = Chancellor of the Exchequer):

1735–42	Sir Robert Walpole (PM, FL, CE)
1742–4	Samuel Sandys (CE until 1743)
1745–53	Earl of Lincoln
1753–4	Lewis Watson
1754–61	Hon. Henry Bilson-Legge (CE)
1762	Thomas Pelham
1762–3	Sir Francis Dashwood (CE)
1763–5	George Grenville (PM, FL, CE)
1765–6	William Dowdeswell (CE)
1766–7	Hon. Charles Townshend (CE)
1767–82	Lord North (CE; PM, FL 1770–82)
1782	Lord John Cavendish (CE)
1782–3	William Pitt (CE)
1783	Duke of Portland (PM, FL)
1783–1801	William Pitt (PM, FL, CE)
1801–4	Henry Addington (PM, FL, CE)
1804–6	William Pitt (PM, FL, CE)
1806–7	Lord Grenville (PM, FL)
1807	Duke of Portland (PM, FL)
1807–12	Spencer Perceval (CE; PM, FL 1809–12)
1812–23	Nicholas Vansittart (CE)
1823–7	F.J. Robinson (CE)
1827	George Canning (PM, FL, CE)
1827–8	Lord Goderich (PM, FL)
1828–30	Duke of Wellington (PM, FL)
1830	Earl Bathurst
1830–4	Earl Grey (PM, FL)

For many years No. 10 was used either as a residence for officials, generally the Prime Minister's private secretary, or simply as offices, with the state rooms being brought into service for official occasions. From 1847 to 1877 it had no tenant.

1877–80	Benjamin Disraeli (PM, FL)
1880–5	W.E. Gladstone (PM, FL; CE 1880–2)
1885–6	Sir Stafford Northcote (FL)
1886	W.E. Gladstone (PM, FL)
1886–91	W.H. Smith (FL)
1891–2	A.J. Balfour (FL)
1892–4	W.E. Gladstone (PM, FL)
1894	Earl of Rosebery (PM)
1895–1905	A.J. Balfour (FL; PM 1902–5)

All Prime Ministers since Balfour have lived at No. 10 and they have all been First Lords of the Treasury. None of them has combined the office of Prime Minister with that of Chancellor of the Exchequer.

1905–8	Sir Henry Campbell-Bannerman
1908–16	H.H. Asquith
1916–22	David Lloyd George
1922–3	A. Bonar Law
1923–4	Stanley Baldwin
1924	Ramsay MacDonald
1924–9	Stanley Baldwin
1929–35	Ramsay MacDonald
1935–7	Stanley Baldwin
1937–40	Neville Chamberlain
1940–5	Winston Churchill
1945–51	Clement Attlee
1951–5	Winston Churchill
1955–7	Sir Anthony Eden
1957–63	Harold Macmillan (three years were spent at Admiralty House while No. 10 was being extensively repaired)
1963–4	Sir Alec Douglas-Home
1964–70	Harold Wilson
1970–4	Edward Heath
1974–6	Harold Wilson (No. 10 was only used for official purposes)
1976–9	James Callaghan
1979–	Mrs Margaret Thatcher

BIBLIOGRAPHY

Works consulted included:

A Churchill Family Album, Mary Soames (Allen Lane, 1982).
An Encyclopaedia of Parliament, Norman Wilding and Philip Laundy (Cassell, 1972).
Downing Street Diary. The Macmillan Years, 1957/63, Harold Evans (Hodder & Stoughton, 1981).
Dublin from Downing Street, John Peck (Gill & Macmillan, 1978).
Foot-Prints in Time. Memories, John Colville (Collins, 1976).
Lloyd George Was My Father, Olwen Carey Evans, as told to Mary Garner (Gomer Press, 1985).
Lloyd George. A Diary, Frances Stevenson, edited by A.J.P. Taylor (Hutchinson, 1971).
Margot. A Life of the Countess of Oxford and Asquith, Daphne Bennett (Gollancz, 1984).
Mr Churchill's Secretary, Elizabeth Nel (Hodder & Stoughton, 1958).
My Darling Pussy. The Letters of Lloyd George and Frances Stevenson, 1931–41 (Weidenfeld & Nicolson, 1975).
No. 10 Downing Street, Whitehall, Charles Eyre Pascoe (Duckworth, 1908).
No. 10 Downing Street, Basil Fuller and John Cornes (Stanley Paul, 1936).
No. 10 Downing Street, 1660–1900, Hector Bolitho (Hutchinson, 1957).
No. 10 Downing Street. A House in History, R.J. Minney (Cassell, 1963).
No. 10 Downing Street, John Charlton, MVO, FSA (HMSO, 1977).
No. 10 Downing Street, John Charlton (HMSO, 1984).
Number 10. The Private Lives of Six Prime Ministers, Terence Feely (Sidgwick & Jackson, 1983).
Old and New London, Edward Walford (Cassell, Petter, Galpin).
Parliament Past and Present, Arnold Wright and Philip Smith (Hutchinson, 1902).
Royal Westminster, Penelope Hunting (RICS, 1981).
Sibley's Harvard Graduates. Class of 1642, Charles William Sever (Cambridge, Mass., 1873).
Survey of London, Montagu H. Cox and Philip Norman (London County Council, 1931).
10 Downing Street, Egon Jameson (Francis Aldor, 1945).
Thatcher, The First Term, Patrick Cosgrave (The Bodley Head, 1985).
The Autobiography of Margot Asquith, edited by Mark Bonham Carter (Eyre and Spottiswoode, 1962).
The Diary of Samuel Pepys, edited by Robert Latham and William Matthews (Bell, 1977–).
The Dictionary of National Biography.

The History of the King's Works, gen. ed. H.M. Colvin, Vols V & VI (1976, 1973).
The Mirrors of Downing Street, by 'A Gentleman with a Duster' (Mills & Boon, 1920).
The Wives of Downing Street, Kirsty McLeod (Collins, 1976).
Winston Churchill, Henry Pelling (Macmillan, 1974).

ACKNOWLEDGEMENTS

It is always a privilege to be invited into anyone's house. It is a particular privilege to be invited into the Prime Minister's house at No. 10 Downing Street. I am, therefore, especially grateful to the Prime Minister not only for allowing my colleagues and myself into both the private and the official sections of her home, but also for the zestful enthusiasm with which she gave us her valuable time to make the two BBC programmes on which this book is based. I am especially grateful for the preface which she has generously provided for this book.

My gratitude must also extend to the staff at No. 10. To Robin Butler, the Principal Private Secretary; to Bernard Ingham, the Prime Minister's Chief Press Secretary; to Jean Caines, the Deputy Chief Press Secretary, who coped so amiably with much of the complexity of the long filming process; and to all the other staff at No. 10 who allowed us to interrupt their immensely busy and complex lives.

I would like to thank, too, the former Prime Ministers, and their wives, who so willingly recalled for us their days in Downing Street: Lord and Lady Home; Lord and Lady Wilson; Lady Avon; Mr Heath; and Mr and Mrs Callaghan. We invaded their present homes and took up so much of their time, and I am most grateful for their willing co-operation.

My gratitude extends, also, to many former members of the staff at No. 10, and to members of the families of former Prime Ministers, all of whom so willingly relived for us their most precious memories of their days in this historic house. I would like to thank, too, John Charlton for his wise and patient historical guidance.

For myself, my personal thanks to the colleagues with whom I had the privilege to work when we made the BBC television programmes. Chiefly, of course, to Jenny Barraclough, the endlessly patient and efficient producer, and to her assistant, Sally Benge; to the film cameraman, Jim Peirson, and his crew; to Robert Hill, the photographer who took many of the pictures in this in this book; and to Vanessa Whinney who once again so ably found the pictures.

My thanks must also go to Tony Kingsford, the editor of this book, whose sharp and informed eye has rescued me from many a gauche slip-up.

I trust that this book will have done at least something to explain to the people on whose behalf No. 10 exists something of what goes on behind that famous front door.

PICTURE CREDITS

Page numbers in bold type denote colour photographs. Picture research by Vanessa Whinney.

Pages 8 Guildhall Library; 10 Ashmolean Museum, Oxford; 13, 16 Fotomas Index; 17 From Pascoe: *No. 10 Downing Street* (1908); 18 Guildhall Library; 21 From *Survey of London* (1931), Courtesy of B. T. Batsford Ltd; 22 *left* Baron George de Dozsa. Photo National Portrait Gallery; 22 *right* National Portrait Gallery; 23, 24 BBC Hulton Picture Library; 27 British Museum; 29 Downing College, Cambridge. Photo Michael Manni; 30 Fotomas Index; 31 BBC Hulton Picture Library; **33** *above* Guildhall Library/Bridgeman Art Library; **33** *below* Government Art Collection. Photo Eileen Tweedy; **34** *both above* Private Collection; **34** *below* National Portrait Gallery; **35** Birmingham Museums and Art Gallery; **36** Downing College, Cambridge. Photo Michael Manni; **37** *above* Reproduced by Gracious Permission of Her Majesty The Queen; **37** *below* Fotomas Index; **38** Government Art Collection. Photos Eileen Tweedy; **39** The Marquis of Cholmondeley; **40** *above* Government Art Collection. Photo Eileen Tweedy; **40** *below* Reproduced by Gracious Permission of Her Majesty The Queen; 42 British Library; 45 Devonshire Collection, Chatsworth. Reproduced by permission of the Chatsworth Settlement Trustees. Photo Courtauld Institute; 46 From *Survey of London* (1931), Courtesy of B. T. Batsford Ltd; 48 Guildhall Library; 53 From Pascoe: *No. 10 Downing Street* (1908); 56 Mansell Collection; **57** British Museum/Fotomas Index; **58** The Society of Dilettanti; **59** *above* Museum of London; **59** *below* Government Art Collection. Photo Leger Gallery; **60** *above* Westminster Library. Photo Godfrey New; **60** *below* National Portrait Gallery; **61** *above left* Reproduced by Gracious Permission of Her Majesty The Queen; **61** *above right* National Portrait Gallery; **61** *below* Government Art Collection. Photo Eileen Tweedy; **62** The Greater London Council as Trustees of the Iveagh Bequest, Kenwood; **63** *left* Photo Robert Hill; **63** *right* Library of Congress, Washington DC. Photo Philip de Bay; **64** British Museum. Photo ET Archive; 69, 70 BBC Hulton Picture Library; 71 British Museum; 74, 77 *left* BBC Hulton Picture Library; 77 *right* National Portrait Gallery; 80 Christ Church, Oxford; **81** Palace of Westminster. Photo Godfrey New; **82** *above* Westminster Library. Photo Godfrey New; **82** *below left* Guildhall Library/Bridgeman Art Library; **82** *below right* Westminster Library. Photo Godfrey New; **83** British Museum/Fotomas Index; **84** National Portrait Gallery; **85** Sir John Soane's Museum; **86** Private collection of the Duke of Wellington. Photo Eileen Tweedy; **87** Fotomas Index; **88** *above* Laing Art Gallery, Newcastle-upon-Tyne; **88** *below*, 90 National Portrait Gallery; 93 BBC Hulton Picture Library; 94 National Portrait Gallery; 95 *above* Westminster Library; 95 *below*, 98 *above* BBC Hulton Picture Library; 98 *below* Westminster Library; 100 BBC Hulton Picture Library; 103 *left* Westminster Library; 103 *right* Government Art Collection. Photo Robert Hill; 104, 105 BBC Hulton

Picture Library; 106, 107 *above* Westminster Library; 107 *below* BBC Hulton Picture Library; 108 *above* Westminster Library; 108 *below* BBC Hulton Picture Library; 109 *left* Mansell Collection; 109 *right* Illustrated London News Picture Library; 110 *all four* BBC Hulton Picture Library; 111 Illustrated London News Picture Library; 114 Weidenfeld & Nicolson Ltd; 115, 116 BBC Hulton Picture Library; 117 *above* Illustrated London News Picture Library; 117 *below*, 118, 119, 120 BBC Hulton Picture Library; **121** National Portrait Gallery; **122** *above* National Liberal Club. Photo Godfrey New; **122** *below*, 123 National Portrait Gallery; **124**, 125 *above* From Pascoe: *No. 10 Downing Street* (1908); **125** *both below* Westminster Library. From Philip Norman; *London Vanished and Vanishing* (1905); **126, 127** National Portrait Gallery; **128** *above* Government Art Collection. Photo Eileen Tweedy; **128** *below* St Stephen's Constitutional Club. Photo Eileen Tweedy; 129, 130 BBC Hulton Picture Library; 131 Associated Press; 133 *above* Topham; 133 *below*, 134, 135 BBC Hulton Picture Library; 136 *above, centre, below right* Imperial War Museum; 136 *below left* Mansell Collection; 138 Cecil Beaton photograph, courtesy of Sotheby's, London; 139 Illustrated London News Picture Library; 140 Imperial War Museum; 141 BBC Hulton Picture Library; 143 Illustrated London News Picture Library; 144 Photo-Source/Illustrated London News Picture Library; **145** *left* National Portrait Gallery; **145** *right* University of Birmingham; **146** National Portrait Gallery; **147** Press Association; **148** Private Collection/ Illustrated London News Picture Library; **149** Department of the Environment; **150, 151, 152** National Portrait Gallery; 153 Press Association/Illustrated London News Picture Library; 154 *left* Associated Press; 154 *above right* BBC Hulton Picture Library; 154 *below right* Topham; 155 *above* Keystone Press Agency Ltd; 155 *below left* BBC Hulton Picture Library; 155 *below right*, 156 *above* Topham; 156 *below left* Photo-Source/Illustrated London News Picture Library; 156 *below right* Photo-Source; 157 BBC Hulton Picture Library; 159 Press Association; **161, 162** *above left* Photo Robert Hill; **162** *above right* Department of the Environment; **162** *below left* Photo Robert Hill; **162** *below right* Photo Eileen Tweedy; **163** *both* Photo Robert Hill; **164** *above* Private Collection. Photo Eileen Tweedy; **164** *below* Photo Robert Hill; **165** *above* Department of the Environment; **165** *both below* Photo Robert Hill; **166** *above* Department of the Environment; **166** *all below*, **167, 168, 169** Photo Robert Hill; **170** Department of the Environment; **171** *above* Photo Dagmar L. Galt, Office of the Prime Minister of Canada; **171** *below* Department of the Environment; **172, 173, 174** Photo Robert Hill; **175** *above* Department of the Environment; **175** *below* Photo Robert Hill; **176** *above left* Department of the Environment; **176** *above right, below* Photo Robert Hill; 181 BBC Hulton Picture Library.

INDEX

Page numbers in *italic* refer to the illustrations